PI**TCH** TO WIN

The internationally acclaimed 6-step formula

How To Present, Persuade And Close The Deal

JUSTIN COHEN

Published by Mercury
an imprint of Burnet Media

•

Burnet Media is the publisher of Mercury, Two Dogs
and Two Pups books
info@burnetmedia.co.za   www.burnetmedia.co.za
PO Box 53557, Kenilworth, 7745, South Africa

•

First published 2018
1 3 5 7 9 8 6 4 2

•

Publication © 2018 Burnet Media
Text © 2018 Justin Cohen
Author portrait © Melissa Hogarth

•

•

Distributed by Jacana Media
www.jacana.co.za

•

Printed and bound by ABC Press
www.abcpress.co.za

•

ISBN 9781928230588

Also available in ebook

Set in PMN Caecilia Pro 9.75pt

About The Author

Justin Cohen is an international speaker, trainer and bestselling author with a postgraduate degree in psychology. He is a world-leading expert on pitching for business, and has coached entrepreneurs, small businesses and major corporates to win some of the toughest multimillion-dollar deals. He has spoken in more than 20 countries to numerous Fortune 500 companies, including Barclays, BMW, Duke, EY, HSBC, Mercedes-Benz, Microsoft, Walmart and Virgin.

Justin is a Speaker Hall of Fame inductee and has hosted various TV shows, including *Gurus With Justin Cohen* on CNBC Africa.

See more about him at www.justinpresents.com.

To all my wonderful clients.
You pushed me to pitch better, then
you pushed me to teach you how.
Thank you.

Without you there would be no
Pitch To Win.

CONTENTS ....

INTRODUCTION

Have you ever been convinced that what you were offering was the best possible option?

Maybe you just knew you were the right person for the job. Or you had a winning product that would undoubtedly sell, or a service that everyone would love. And you didn't just know it in your heart, you knew it in your head. Apples for apples, your value proposition was better.

Yet after submitting your proposal and delivering your pitch those sickening words landed in your inbox: 'We regret to inform you...' Or worse, they didn't even bother to let you know.

I know what it's like. For years I struggled to close deals. I'd go in, have a great conversation with a potential client, feel sure I had it in the bag – then lose the business to a competitor, often someone offering less value at a higher price.

I remember the day I finally got my wakeup call. I'd just lost a five-figure deal to exactly that: someone offering

'There is only one valid definition of business purpose: to create a customer.'

– Peter Drucker

less value at a higher price! Working my frustration out at the gym, it hit me: offering great value isn't enough.

It's not enough to have the best product; you've got to have the best pitch.

BUILD IT AND THEY <u>WON'T</u> COME

Remember the immortal idea from Kevin Costner's *Field of Dreams?* 'If you build it, they will come'? It's a lie.

If you build it – and here's the kicker – *if you pitch it better than anyone else*, then and only then, will they come (maybe).

If you're anything like me, you're passionate about your products and services. You want to make a real difference in your customer's lives. You've spent a lifetime going from good to great. News flash: great is not good enough.

For real business success, it's not good enough to be great at what you do. You have to be great at *pitching* what you do. In fact, you have to be *even better at pitching what you do* than doing what you do.

You may think that sucks. I did! All I wanted to do was create and deliver. But that's a fantasy – one you'll see in *Field of Dreams*. Reality is different.

In reality it's not the best product that wins; it's the best pitch.

Imagine bringing a life-saving drug into the world. Surely you wouldn't have to market that? News would spread like wildfire. Sick people would be beating your door down! Wrong.

According to *The Washington Post*, pharmaceutical companies spend more on pitching their drugs than on research and development. If it's like that for a cure for cancer, why should it be any different for what you and I have to offer?

No wonder that a series of studies on the buying behaviour of more than 100,000 decision-makers found that nearly 40 percent of business-to-business buyers select a vendor based on the skills of the person making the pitch rather than price, quality or service.[1]

DISCOVERING A WINNING FORMULA

Once I had accepted reality, I spent the next three-and-a-half years immersing myself in every book and programme I could find on sales and marketing. At first I did it purely as a means to an end. My mission is to equip and inspire individuals and organisations to realise their potential, which I do through the various books and programmes that I've produced. If fulfilling my mission required getting good at pitching, then I would get good at pitching, whether I hated it or not. But something unexpected happened.

The more I dug in, the more I realised that pitching was just communicating and educating. And I love communicating and educating.

Ever got fired up telling someone about what you do? That's the basis of a great pitch. As I started to apply the method, my business exploded. I even pitched and won my own CNBC Africa talk show, *Gurus With Justin Cohen*, where I interview leading experts on success.

BUT WILL IT WORK FOR EVERYONE?

I hadn't intended to share my developing pitching method until one day I got a call from IBM. The multinational giant runs one of the biggest entrepreneurship competitions in the world, the IBM Global Entrepreneur of the Year awards, and they wanted me to deliver the keynote presentation at the African leg of the competition. Afterwards, they asked me to coach the African finalists, a small startup from Kenya called Mode.

They had a great business but they were pitching it like many startups do, with reams of boring facts and the endless PowerPoint deck. (For businesspeople, our PowerPoint slides are like our children: no matter how ugly they are, we still think they're beautiful!) After applying the Pitch To Win method that I had developed for my own business, Mode went on to win not only the semifinals in Brazil, but also the finals in New York, beating top startups from all over the world. Their CEO was kind enough to give this method part of the credit for their win.

(We'll get back to the Mode pitch in some detail a little later.)

I still hadn't seriously considered offering my pitching strategies as a service until I was asked to deliver the keynote presentation at an international conference for EY (Ernst & Young), one of the Big Four accounting firms. Afterwards their CEO called me to ask if I would coach a team that had a major pitch coming up, to one of the world's largest banks.

It turned out to be a multimillion-dollar deal – but when I arrived on the scene, the prospects didn't look good. EY's UK office had recently lost the European business and now the pressure was on the African office to win it. As a result of the bank's strong relationship with the incumbent service provider, one of the senior partners I found myself dealing with believed they had no more than a 20 percent chance of success. I was nervous. It's a stereotype, but accountants generally aren't renowned as scintillating communicators. (If an accountant's wife can't fall asleep, she says to her husband, tell me about your day...)

The team diligently applied the Pitch To Win formula. The big day arrived. After the pitch there was dead silence. And then the selection committee did something they'd never done before. They applauded.

When I got that news, it became clear to me. Pitching was not an inborn talent. It was a skill that just about anyone could acquire. Even accountants!

Having won the business, I was asked to codify the methodology that I had used so that it could be rolled out through the business. I had never thought about making this an official part of my offering, because I hadn't worked out how it would enable me to fulfil my purpose. But I finally got it. If my mission was to help people be their best but they didn't have the best pitch, they wouldn't realise their potential and I wouldn't fulfil my mission.

Having spent two years to that point developing my programme for my own use, it was time to make the Pitch To Win formula available to everyone. I have now been teaching pitching for years, all over the world. For so many people who have everything else in place, I have seen that this is often the missing key that unlocks their success.

I PITCH. YOU PITCH. WE ALL PITCH

Any time you influence anyone to do anything – hire you, promote you, marry you – you're pitching them on a course of action. If you can't pitch you can't influence, and if you can't influence you're powerless. The greater the difference you want to make in the world, the greater the pitch you need to be able to make. Gandhi, Mandela, Mother Teresa – these icons made a difference because they knew how to *pitch* to people about the difference they wanted to make.

You are holding in your hand the blueprint to a winning pitch. May you use it to pitch your difference so that you can make an even bigger difference!

EMBRACING A GROWTH MINDSET – USING THIS BOOK

You know those kids at school who didn't have to work hard and got straight As? I had to work really hard for a D. I was convinced I just wasn't born with enough talent or intelligence. In fact, this belief may have been the very thing holding me back.

Research shows that when you're learning a new language, sport or subject, your belief about your ability has a greater impact on your success than almost anything else. Professor Carol Dweck of Stanford University calls it the difference between a **fixed mindset** and a **growth mindset**. [2]

Those with a fixed mindset believe that talent, ability and intelligence are inborn. You either have it or you don't. People with this mindset not only learn less but they show poorer problem-solving ability and are more likely to give up. Incredibly, if you prime anyone with this mindset, just by praising them for being smart or talented, you will actually reduce their IQ. Why? Because when you imply that our talent is inborn we don't want to prove you wrong, so we're less creative and take fewer risks, which in turn reduces our ability.

In contrast, Dweck has found that those with a growth mindset believe that talent and ability are something that you acquire through hard work and application. These people are not afraid to take on new challenges and fail, because they know that's how you improve. They're focused not on *proving* their ability but *growing* their ability.

In fact, a growth mindset is far closer to the truth. The Swedish psychologist Anders Ericsson has spent decades studying ability. His research has shown that inborn factors are not responsible for expert level mastery in almost every field. So what is? Practice.

Top musicians practise around a third more than average ones. Not just any practice though, *deliberate* practice. By that, Ericsson means getting outside your comfort zone and trying new things, establishing well-defined learning goals and receiving feedback from a teacher.[3]

So, here is how to get the most out of this book:

1 Recognise that the ability to pitch is not inborn; it is acquired.
2 Be willing to try and fail; that's how we grow.
3 Practise pitching as much as possible.
4 Establish clear goals; for example, building your confidence.

5 Seek feedback from partners or team members.
6 Realise that everyone can learn to be great at
pitching.
7 Have fun!

Given that the best way to learn is to do,
I strongly recommend that, as you learn about each
aspect of a winning pitch, you apply it in practice.
Ideally, film yourself. In the extensive training and
coaching I do on this programme, I find that the
most valuable learning comes from people seeing
themselves in action. You'll almost immediately
see what needs to be improved.

Now, let's get pitching!

TUNE IN ············

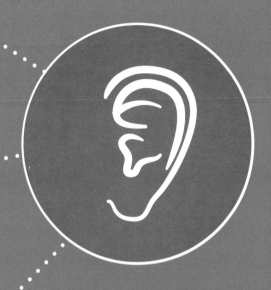

CHAPTER 1

T UNE IN

'Those who listen best win.'

There are six key elements to pitching. The first, **Tuning In**, is the critical starting point that I realised my programme was missing only after I had developed the rest of it.

I was coaching a team preparing for a multimillion-dollar pitch. As we were talking ourselves through the pitch I realised we were putting the cart before the horse. The team had a great standard offering but there was an undeniable problem: they weren't clear whether this was what the potential client actually needed. As a result, we changed tack and I spent two days preparing them not for the pitch itself but for a pre-pitch meeting.

We think of a pitch as a performance, and to some degree it is, but this is not a repeat performance like a Broadway play. Every pitch is different because each person or organisation you're pitching to is different.

As a result, the pitch is generally won before you pitch. It's won in how well you understand what the people you're pitching to really want and need, so that you can tailor your pitch accordingly.

You can deliver an outstanding performance but if you don't talk to their needs, their objectives, their pain, that performance is unlikely to earn you a standing ovation.

THEY DON'T CARE ABOUT YOU

If you have a pen nearby, put it behind your ear. Go on. I won't judge you. Now imagine that pen is an antenna. Everyone has one and it's tuned into one station – WIIFM – What's In It For Me?

It may sound harsh but the businesses you pitch to don't really care about you, your company or your list of features and benefits. They care about themselves. They care about their needs, their desires and their pain. Where you and your offering can help them meet those needs, that's where they're interested – but you can't show them that until you've taken the time to listen to what their needs are.

Ideally, you will get the chance to meet them before you pitch. In that session you should do little more than ask questions and listen. Resist the temptation to start selling, to show off your great offering. Selling without understanding what they want is like playing Russian roulette: you might get lucky but you're more likely to kill the deal.

If you don't have the opportunity to meet them beforehand, you will really need to do your homework. With Google it's easy to get started. Find out as much as you can about the company and the specific people you're meeting. If you have any mutual connections, call them up to see what other information you can find. But the real assessment will be face to face. If you have just one meeting, you will need to use the first part of it to figure out where they're at.

I regularly pitch to be the keynote speaker at conferences. I'm usually given just one meeting. I use the first part of the meeting to figure out the client's objectives. They will often ask me to jump straight in and start talking about my offering. Resist the temptation!

Instead, I reply something along these lines: 'Thanks so much for the opportunity to share what I have to offer, but first I'd like to understand what you want to achieve.'

They are usually thrilled to start talking. Remember: they don't really care about me. They care about themselves. In our time-pressed, high-pressure world almost no-one else is giving them the chance to really focus on themselves and their challenges.

Think of yourself as a doctor. You can't prescribe treatment until you've done a diagnosis. This pre-pitch meeting is your chance to diagnose.

If your doctor wrote a prescription without assessing you first, you wouldn't trust him. Same with the people you're pitching to. Besides getting the information you need, listening conveys understanding and interest. That builds trust, which gives you a head start when you get to the pitch itself.

If you are an entrepreneur looking for investors, you might think it's one size fits all. You have a particular business which you need to pitch, and either the investor is going to like it or not. Yes and no. Yes, it's a question of finding the right fit. And yet each investor is different. For some it may be more about the return; for others about disrupting an industry. To each of those people you will have to emphasise different points.

Know thy audience!

Establishing Rapport

It can take a while for people to open up. They need to feel safe so they can trust you. Before you dive straight into your diagnosis, it's useful to establish rapport by getting to know one another.

In a series of negotiation studies carried out between MBA students of two business schools, one group was told: 'Time is money, get straight down to business.' Around 55 percent of those in this group were able to come to an agreement.

A second group was told: 'Before you begin negotiating, exchange some personal information with each other and identify similarities you have in common, *then* begin negotiating.' In this group, 90 percent of participants were able to come to a successful agreement. These agreements were also more likely to result in a win-win outcome.[1]

We tend to do this naturally when we meet people. We may talk about current events, sport or which school or university we went to. This might seem trivial but, as those negotiation studies demonstrate, they are a powerful way to create connection. Some people call this small talk, but small talk is a good stepping stone to big talk!

Similar Social Styles

Another way to boost rapport is to adapt your social style to the style of the person you're talking to. That's why many sales programmes have an element of personality profiling. The idea is that if you can figure out your prospects' personality style, and match it, they are more likely to warm to you.

The risk is that in trying to profile them you could lose focus on the content of what they're saying. Besides, no personality-profiling system captures the full variety of human diversity. So the good news is I'm not going to recommend you learn a complex, on-the-spot profiling method. There is a much easier way to connect with the person you need to influence.

Mirroring

Milton Erickson, one of the fathers of hypnotherapy, discovered that mirroring his client's behavioural patterns by subtly matching their volume, pace, facial expressions or gestures increased the chances of their following his suggestions. This is based on a simple truth: people like people who are like them.

Think about it. If you're soft-spoken, you probably think of yourself as modest and reserved, while people who speak at a much higher volume come across as overbearing and pushy. If you're naturally loud, you may well think of that guy you have to lean in to hear as mousy or a pushover. Notice how two people can frame the same characteristic as either positive or negative, depending on whether they're the ones who possess it. In short, the best kind of people are like us!

But mirroring is about more than liking, it's about trust. I won't follow you if I don't trust you. Because I trust myself, I figure that if you're like me, you're probably trustworthy.

We like people who are like us even in superficial ways. People with similar names – 'Brenda and Brendan, Justin and Justine' – are significantly more likely to marry than chance would have it. People named Jack are four times more likely to move to Jacksonville than people called Philip, who are more likely to move to Philadelphia. You're almost twice as likely to become a dentist if your name is Dennis. [2]

This may all sound a little absurd, but remember, human beings are rationalising rather than rational creatures. We will rationalise our decisions after making them on an emotional impulse. Fortunately, you don't have to pretend that you have the same name as your prospective client! There are far more powerful ways to mirror.

Without determining their personality, all you need to do to influence someone is attune your awareness and subtly mirror their vocal pitch, volume or rhythm, their facial expressions, body language or even what they're saying. Later, when we look at non-verbal communication, we'll discuss ways of doing this.

If mirroring seems disingenuous, remember that we all do it anyway. Watch two people in conversation and you will notice a natural mimicry that emerges when rapport is established. We think of ourselves as self-contained individuals, but actually we are way more interconnected than we realise. We naturally mirror the behaviour and emotions of the people around us. Researchers at the Boston University Medical School have found that as people get deeper into conversation they begin to unconsciously synchronise speech rhythms, finger movements, eye blink rate and even certain brain waves.

Mirroring isn't just a persuasion technique; it enables us to better understand what others are feeling. As we take on their facial expressions, tone of voice or body language, our internal experience begins to match theirs. By feeling what they feel we are better able to respond appropriately. Notice that if you're talking to someone who is sad, initially you will tend to hunch your shoulders and furrow your brow just like them – this helps you empathise. One of the reasons people with autism don't function well socially is that they don't naturally mirror and so they're unable to read people's facial expressions. Their social perception increases as they are taught to mirror.

Mirroring is a natural consequence of relating to others, but research has shown that if we want to build our influence, we need to be more deliberate about it.

- Negotiators who consciously mimicked their opponent's mannerisms were more likely to create a deal that benefited both parties.
- Retail salespeople who were instructed to mirror the facial expressions and body language of their customers achieved nearly 20 percent more sales.
- We can also mirror verbal content. A Dutch study found that waitresses who repeated diners' orders word for word earned 70 percent more tips.[3]

When it comes to rapport building, who mirrors whom? Initially people of lower status tend to mirror those of higher. When you're pitching you generally have lower status, so as a rule you will be mirroring them. However, if you are effective in building rapport, they will start mirroring you too, demonstrating that you have gained status and that they value you and your offering.

MIRRORING AND LEADING

One way to figure out if you are building rapport is to try some *mirroring and leading*. You start mirroring them but then you subtly move in a different direction and see if they follow. If they do, you know you're connecting.

In a pitch, mirroring and leading are more likely to happen verbally. Let's say someone questions your experience. 'I'm not sure you have the experience for this,' she may say. If you immediately contradict her and start listing the projects you've worked on, she may feel undermined and discount what you've said. However, if you first *mirror* her concern by paraphrasing what she's said, you can then *lead* her into another perspective. You might say, 'You're quite right to be concerned about depth of experience – it's critical to us in delivering on the success of this project. Fortunately I have worked on a number of projects in this field, including…'

If you're selling a premium product, you could position you and your product as the prize to which your prospective client should aspire. I have a private banking client that sells VIP banking services. They make it clear that their product isn't for everyone, and the resulting aura of exclusivity creates desire. I've noticed that some of their top salespeople will almost immediately get their prospective clients to start mirroring them, suggesting that they have claimed the higher-status position. However, we need to be careful with this approach as we could come across as arrogant, a potential turn-off. Personally, I aim for an equal, rather than a higher or lower, status.

Power Listening

Ultimately, tuning in effectively depends on the quality of our listening. Listening means more than waiting for your turn to speak. Once you get to your diagnosis you need to start employing *power listening*. There are three steps:

'Don't listen to reply, listen to understand.'

1 Ask open-ended questions. You can't listen if they're not saying anything. Closed-ended questions, such as 'Are you happy with your current service provider?' lead to a yes or no answer. Open-ended questions, such as 'Can you tell me about your experience with your current service provider?' get them to tell you a story. The more they speak, the better your diagnosis will be, and the better the solution you can provide. Examples of other good open-ended questions are:

- What are the biggest challenges you're facing?
- What do you want to achieve?
- What are your main reasons for investing/ changing suppliers?

2 **Listen** with positive, open body language. It's useful to make notes while they are talking, but be sure to look up often and make eye contact that conveys your positive interest. If they feel they are not being listened to or that you're distracted, they will clam up. (See more on this under 'Body Language' on p73.)

3 **Paraphrase** back what you've heard. If most people were honest, once they were finished talking about themselves they'd say, 'I've spoken enough about me, now *you* talk about me!' This also achieves three important things.

- It clarifies whether you have fully understood them. We can speak the same language but interpret a different meaning. Paraphrasing back ensures you're on the same page and that you can come up with an accurate diagnosis.

- It helps *them* see the problem. Only when they're clear about the problem themselves will they be ready to hear about your solution. Sometimes the only thing you need to do to help someone is listen.
- Finally, it makes them feel that you understand them, which builds your connection. Remember how mirroring builds rapport? Here you are mirroring back content.

Of course, one of the main points of the pre-pitch meeting is for you to gather relevant information to incorporate into your pitch. Look out for any key words or phrases. Use their language in the pitch. The more they feel that you really understand who they are and what they want, the more likely you are to win. A large part of the pitch itself is step three of the Power Listening process – paraphrasing their thoughts and ideas. Tell them what they told you in your initial meeting, and they will listen. The difference is that you will also link their problem to a solution: whatever it is you're offering.

The power of the pre-pitch meeting was brought home to me several years ago after I pitched to what has become a major client of mine. I had an extensive pre-pitch meeting and then in the pitch I spoke to many of the company's key challenges and concerns. Afterwards the MD said to me, 'How did you know so much about us?' Of course he had told me everything in the first meeting; he just hadn't remembered.

One of the greatest misconceptions about the best salespeople is that they're big-talking extroverts. In fact, research shows that the best salespeople are not extroverts or introverts, they're ambiverts – exactly in between. They are people who can listen as well as they can talk. [4]

WHAT A PITCH REALLY IS

Boil your pitch down to its essence and you'll see that what you're really pitching is a *solution* to a *problem*. No-one's going to say to you, my life is perfect, now let me pay you to change it.

Often people don't know they have a problem. I do a lot of work in the financial services industry. These guys are pitching investments and insurance to people who often don't realise they need either. Of course, without these products they almost certainly will have a problem in the future.

Later you will see that a big part of the pitch is highlighting the problem. The best way to do that is to get them to discover the problem themselves by asking the right questions. In the insurance industry

'Pitch to the pain'

it might be as simple as asking, 'If something were to happen to you that prevented you from working, what would happen to your family?' Realising that their family could be left destitute, they will be far more receptive to hearing about life insurance.

If you were trying to get someone to move their business to you, you could ask, 'Is there anything that frustrates you about your current product/ service?' If you power listen correctly, they will become focused on the problem, which will put them in the best possible state to hear about your solution.

TUNE IN

TEAM

O
P
P
S

CHAPTER 2

(T)EAM

'A pitch isn't won by one.'

A few years back, I was brought in to coach a high-level team a week before they pitched for a game-changing international deal. Those involved had gathered from around the world for final rehearsals in Johannesburg. The pressure was on. Reputations and incomes were at stake. One of the first things I picked up on was the underlying tensions among the team. With different members holding different views on how to proceed, stress levels were headed to boiling point and simmering conflicts looked set to explode.

I had a single day with the team, and I spent the entire morning doing nothing but team-building. By the afternoon, everyone was relaxed, smiling and praising each other, and able to agree on how to move forward. I believe that four-hour team build saved the deal.

The relationship between team members is almost as important as the relationship with the client. A strong team raises confidence both internally and externally. Clients sense that if the team gels well in the pitch, they're probably going to gel well throughout the project. There is good evidence for that hunch. A study of sixty different business units found that the most important factor determining the success of a team was how the team members *felt* about one another.[1]

'A team is not a group of people who work together. A team is a group of people who trust each other.'
– Simon Sinek

Even if you pitch alone, the relationships you have with your team back at the office will hugely influence your confidence and competence.

What if two people just don't like each other? Well, most people who get married love each other and yet nearly half of those people end up disliking each other and getting divorced. That tells us that liking isn't determined by who we are but rather what we do. There are two main ways to quickly create affinity: appreciation and self-disclosure.

APPRECIATION

One of the most powerful ways to create affinity is through appreciation. When you express appreciation to me you directly boost my self-esteem and happiness. I associate that good feeling with you, which increases the chances of me wanting to help you. But when you express appreciation for people, you do more than make them feel good; you boost their performance.

Before starting a diagnosis to determine the presence of liver cirrhosis, half of a group of doctors received a small token of appreciation to thank them for their good work. The ones who got the appreciation reached their diagnosis in half the time and were 19 percent more accurate.[2] Moral of the story: if you want an accurate diagnosis, don't wait for your doctor to give you a lollipop, give him one first!

'What gets appreciated gets repeated.' Being appreciated boosts our happiness and happiness boosts our intelligence. Also, there is a fundamental principle of leadership: what gets appreciated gets repeated. When you thank someone for something specific you incentivise them to do it again.

SELF-DISCLOSURE

You can't genuinely like someone if you don't know them. In one team I worked with, which included members who had known each other for twenty years, one didn't know that the other had a daughter with Down's syndrome or that another had briefly been a concert-performing classical pianist. These things may not be directly relevant to getting a job done, but sharing them creates empathy and liking, which is key to a successful team.

Effective teams are made up of people who know, trust and like one another. You won't be able to like someone if you don't trust them, and you can't trust them if you don't know them.

Sharing A Challenge

I once worked with a high-level finance team at a telecoms company. Each person had to tell a story about some challenge they had been through and how they overcame it. They could also talk about a challenge they were currently going through. The challenge could be big or small. There was only one rule: the challenge could not have anything to do with work. The team was so impressed with the results that they started adapting the activity into a weekly exercise. First thing on a Monday, everyone had to share something about themselves that was not work-related.

Six months later my client told me that the performance of the team had risen by 20 percent. Even I was surprised. I asked her to explain why she thought that had happened. She explained that people had generally become more encouraging and supportive, but she gave me one illuminating example. One of the team members was renowned to be tight with budget. It was always a battle to get money out of him. In one of his stories he revealed that he had been an orphan and was often hungry as a child; the little money he was given had to be stretched further than was possible. Suddenly the team realised that this wasn't just a guy being difficult about releasing budget; he was a man who associated spending with loss. Afterwards, when they approached him for budget, instead of emphasising the money they wanted to take, they focused on the need of the person or department the money was going to. He became much more willing to release budget. You can also imagine those conversations being less combative given the empathy that the team now felt for him. That in itself would have made him more receptive to their requests.

Personal story sharing can be a little uncomfortable at first. I've facilitated many of these sessions and on more than one occasion I've seen tears shed, but those participating always feel closer to one another afterwards. And I'm always struck by the uptick in performance. You suddenly gets the sense that, having revealed their vulnerability, this team will now go to war for one another. It's difficult for me to feel empathy for you if all I see is your illusion of invincibility. Of course, each person gets to share no more than they are comfortable with – but usually the more they are prepared to reveal, the more benefit to the team.

The other advantage of personal storytelling is that it provides a vent. If you're dealing with a divorce, a sick child or a cancer scare, it consumes emotional resources. Ever since Freud smoked a pipe, we've known that just talking about something that's bothering you helps to release the emotional distress. Hence his therapy was known as the 'talking cure'.

After listening, Freud would provide an interpretation of what the patient had said. In the 1960s, the American psychotherapist Carl Rogers found that this was not always necessary. The real benefit the patient got was simply having someone listen without judgment. The therapist might ask the occasional question or paraphrase an important point, but the healing would come through talking it out with someone providing what he called 'unconditional positive regard'.[3]

Our aim, of course, is not therapy; it's a high-quality pitch. But for that we need to ensure that everyone is in a peak state to perform. Worrying about moving house or a conflict you're having with your brother can sap resources required for the pitch. Talking about it is not going to make it go away but it will release some of that negative emotional energy and likely elicit valuable support from the team.

TUNE IN
TEAM
OPTIMISM
P
P
S

CHAPTER 3

OPTIMISM

'The most important person you need to pitch is yourself.'

'We regret to inform you...' Don't you hate those words? I used to hear them all too often. It's the main reason why people say they hate sales. What they're really saying is they hate *rejection*.

We are all hard-wired to hate rejection. It stems back to our caveman days, when we would die if our tribe rejected us. This may no longer be true today, but our brains still interpret rejection as a mortal threat.

We've got to get over this rejection thing. Why? Because success lies on the other side of rejection.

It takes between five and twelve exposures to a product, service or idea before people will buy. That's five to twelve rejections before they say yes. The most successful people hear the word 'no' more than anyone. They know, whether consciously or not, that the only way to get to a YES is through those NOs.

In other words, we have to be rejection specialists.

REJECTION VACCINE

A vaccine is like karate training for the immune system. In being exposed to a tiny amount of a disease, the body learns to defend itself against it. If rejection is the disease (dis-ease, as in, it makes us feel uneasy), the best way to defend ourselves against it is to expose ourselves to it. The more we experience it, the more immune we become to it. But if we avoid it at all costs, the more our fear of it grows.

By regularly offering our services through big pitches or small – and experiencing the inevitable rejections that will come – we will find the whole idea less and less scary. The key is to feel the fear and do it any way.

The more you pitch, the less fear you feel.

And the more you pitch, the more likely you are to eventually win. That's just statistics.

THE MINDSET OF THOSE WHO WIN

When researchers want to understand what it takes to be great in sales they usually go to one of the toughest sales industries on the planet: insurance. Here, you have to convince someone to sacrifice part of their salary every month so they can get rich when they have an accident and die! Insurance agents get more rejection then just about any other sales profession. I like to say that insurance is like New York: if you can make it there, you can make it anywhere.

In the mid-'80s, MetLife, one of the largest insurance companies in the world, had a problem shared by many of its competitors. Forget about how to sell the most policies; they couldn't even predict who was going to stick it out in the company. New recruits would become so demoralised by all the rejection they were getting that they would give up almost immediately. The usual predictors of success – IQ, qualifications and personality profiling – were telling them nothing, and the company was losing $75 million a year in wasted hiring costs.

'You think you can, you think you can't, you're always right.'
– Henry Ford

Then enter Dr Martin

Seligman, head of the American Psychological Association. Seligman hypothesised that the star insurance salespeople would mostly be optimists. What is an optimist? An optimist is somebody who expects the best outcome. They will persist through setback and difficulty, driven by the belief that even if things don't work out immediately, eventually, as long as they keep at it, success will likely be theirs. The rational optimist is not optimistic that there won't be a problem; rather she believes she will be able to find a solution when one arises.

MetLife were sceptical but they allowed him to investigate. Amazingly, he found that the most optimistic salespeople were not only more likely to stick it out in the company, but they achieved 56 percent more sales. Optimism was a better predictor of success in sales than IQ, qualifications or work experience. This research has now been replicated across a range of different industries.[1]

OPTIMISM IN THE FACE OF CHALLENGE

Why is optimism so important in sales? Remember, it takes between five and twelve exposures to a new product before a person will buy. We are all basically late adopters, which is another survival instinct. Humans see threats before rewards. If our caveman ancestors ate those luscious red berries the first time they saw them, that might have been the last time they ate anything. Better to take a little time to find out more about those berries. See how they affect other people. The more positive unthreatening exposures we have to a product, service or person, the more likely we are to eventually say yes.

In pitching you are guilty until proven innocent. That means we often need to lose before we win.

'You miss 100% of the shots you don't take.' – Michael Jordan

Sometimes I think this book should have been called *Pitch To Lose And Lose And Lose... So That We Can Eventually Win!*

Yet most salespeople give up after the first call. They assume the first NO they hear means no forever. This becomes a self-fulfilling prophecy because of course if you don't go back and try again, you don't get the deal and you prove yourself right.

By contrast, after a setback the optimist thinks to herself, 'If I stay engaged, learn from my setbacks, adjust my approach, or just give them time to become comfortable with me, eventually I'll get the business.'

There are a few caveats to this thinking. It assumes, for instance, that the prospective client both needs and can afford what you have to offer. And, of course, I'm not talking about calling them 12 times in an hour!

Note also that an exposure isn't only a hard pitch for business. Besides a call, an exposure might be a special offer, a sample or just some useful information that positions you as the authority in your industry. The best kind of exposures are value-based: they give your prospect something they can use, and in the process prove your value to them.

I regularly put out a blog on my website. I give away valuable information. Most of the people who receive my blog will probably never buy anything from me, but there are those who will, and by regularly giving out good, free information I increase the likelihood that they will.

In business, as long as you are providing value, familiarity doesn't breed contempt, it breeds sales.

Optimism is also necessary for your confidence in the pitch. Conviction is contagious. When *you* are absolutely convinced that your offering is the best, there is a much greater chance your clients will be too. That's why the most important person you need to sell is you.

Take a controversial topic such as abortion or capital punishment. Whatever your view, imagine you had to persuade people to believe the opposite view. You might marshal every argument there is, but your lack of conviction would unconsciously seep into your non-verbal communication, undermining your influence. The best way to ensure *their* confidence in your message is to ensure your own.

When you're feeling down about a setback or challenge, shift to optimism by asking yourself two questions. It's helpful to write down the answers you come up with, but even going through them in your mind will help.

1 'What's good about what happened?'
It's not facts but interpretations that make us negative. While you've acknowledged that there is something wrong with the situation, take the opportunity to acknowledge what's right with it. Think about what you can learn from it or how it could make you a better person.

Failure is a great teacher – if we allow ourselves to learn from it. As the Dalai Lama says, 'When you lose, don't lose the lesson.'

2 'What can I do about it?'
We usually only need one solution but come up

with many. It takes lots of potential solutions to find a good one, and cultivating a solution mindset is a key ingredient of success.

The biggest failures never fail, because they never try. These are the naysayers who keep saying, 'It's never going to work!' Of course something will never work if it's never tried, so they land up proving themselves right. How can we win if we don't get on the field? And when we don't win the business, the Dalai Lama again has it right: 'There is always a lesson to win.'

POSITIVITY

Rational optimism differs from positive thinking in that you look for real reasons to back up your positive expectations rather than just blindly taking on a positive attitude. When challenges do arise you don't ignore them, you look for solutions. But even positive thinking has its place.

In an endurance study, cyclists who were subliminally exposed to positive words like 'go' and 'lively' pushed nearly 20 percent harder than those exposed to negative words like 'toil' and 'sleep'.[2] Being exposed to happy instead of sad faces also gave them a significant advantage. There is a direct correlation between positivity and performance.

Express Positive Expectations

Professor Tim Noakes is one of the world's leading exercise and sports scientists. One of his primary research interests is 'brain regulation of exercise performance'. Having extensively studied and worked with a range of sports champions and endurance athletes, Noakes explains that when a fraction of a percentage separates the winner from the runner-up, the critical difference is not physiology, it's belief.

He often cites the example of Roger Bannister, who was the first man to run the four-minute mile. Before he managed this great feat, many experts thought it was impossible. The closest anyone had got was 4:01 minutes, and that was nearly a decade before. There were doctors who thought that pushing the body below four minutes would kill a man. Even Bannister thought it was impossible, but one day before a race, his coach Franz Stampfl said something that changed his mind. He said, 'You can do a 3:56 mile.'

A good coach sees you not as you are, but as you can be. When you trust that person and internalise their belief in you, self-imposed limits can be shattered. Bannister would later explain that everything changed after he heard his coach say those words.

On 6 May 1954, on Iffley Road Track in Oxford, Roger Bannister ran a mile in 3 minutes 59.4 seconds, breaking not only a physical but a mental barrier. Suddenly, it was seen as possible. Six weeks later the Australian John Landy became the second man to do it, and barely a year later three people did it in one race! [3]

The way I see it, the real hero of the four-minute mile was Franz Stampfl, who made one man see that the impossible was possible.

Expressing positive expectations doesn't just boost the performance of athletes, it boosts the performance of accountants. Half a group of new auditors who had recently joined one of the Big Four accounting firms were told that they had been singled out as having high potential to succeed, with the skills to overcome challenges, and that management had high expectations for them. Actually they were considered no better than the auditors in a control group. Yet for a full month afterwards they earned significantly higher performance ratings than those who did not receive this positive feedback. [4]

For pitching, the lesson is simple. During your preparations be sure to express lots of positive expectations, particularly when you're giving feedback.

GIVING FEEDBACK

Throughout your rehearsal process you're going to be giving one another feedback and possibly receiving feedback from external panellists. Feedback is critical for improvement, but if it's given in the wrong way, it can crush optimism and reduce performance. Did you ever receive feedback that made you think to yourself, 'I'm in the wrong job, I'm in the wrong career, I'm in the wrong life...' That's because it left you feeling like there was something wrong with you that you could do nothing about.

The primitive part of the brain sees criticism as a threat that it needs to defend itself against. But this part of the brain doesn't distinguish well between physical and emotional threats. That's why criticism can lead to a shot of stress hormones that raise heart rate, breathing rate and blood pressure. This activates the 'fight or flight' response. In survival mode we are less able to properly process the feedback with the more evolved part of our brain, our neocortex. Instead, we may become defensive.

When you give feedback it's important to see people not as they are but as they can be. It's best to start with positive feedback. This makes the person more motivated to hear what needs to be improved. Also, by affirming what is working you increase the chances of it being repeated. When describing what needs to

'Feedback is the breakfast of champions.'
– Ken Blanchard

be improved don't criticise the person; rather focus on the specific thing that needs to change. Be sure to end with a positive expectation, as simple as 'You can do it!'

I have worked with teams brimming with enthusiasm only to see their spirit crushed by poorly delivered negative feedback. Be sure to brief any internal assessors on this technique. However, we can't always guarantee how feedback will be provided. If you are on the receiving end of some tactless feedback, thank the assessors for their insight, consider whether there is merit in what they're saying, and apply it. But keep your spirits up by reminding yourself of the positives.

In a survey of 70 top European companies on the reasons behind a winning pitch, the number one reason given was energy and enthusiasm.[5] Make sure you keep yours and your team's up with plenty of positivity.

TUNE IN
TEAM
OPTIMISM
PRESENCE
P
S

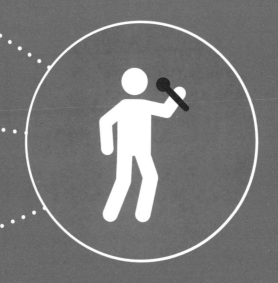

CHAPTER 4

P RESENCE

'Your presence is measured in how people feel in your presence.'

You know those people who walk into a room and the lights go on? You know those people who walk *out* of a room and the lights go on?

What happens when you walk into a room? How do people feel in your presence?

Presence is determined less by what you say and more by *how* you say it. Depending on the context of your message, more than half of its impact likely comes from your non-verbal communication.[1] In fact, one study shows that when verbal and non-verbal communication contradict each other, we are five times more likely to believe the non-verbal signal.[2] The more serious problem, however, is that when our non-verbal communication contradicts our verbal, we are interpreted as confusing, unstable and insincere.

Imagine your partner telling you he or she loves you while looking over your shoulder with folded arms and a distant stare. You might start rethinking your marriage proposal... Likewise, in a pitch your words can make a compelling case, but if you're not perceived as credible and confident, they will not be convincing. Research shows that a lie expressed confidently is more likely to be believed than the truth expressed doubtfully. That's because confidence is one of the ways we assess truth. If you're confident, people assume you believe what you're saying and that makes it more likely to be true.

There is another reason that confidence is critical. We tend to mirror the emotions of the most prominent person near us. While you're speaking you are the leader, and what you are leading more than anything are our emotions. Have you ever sat in a presentation where the presenter seemed uncomfortable and awkward and you found yourself squirming in embarrassment? You were mirroring his discomfort.

Conversely, when a presenter is super-energised and confident you feel the same. So, if you want to know how your audience feels about you... look in the mirror.

Here follow four non-verbal ways to boost your presence.

NON-VERBAL COMMUNICATION

VOICE

Your voice is the music to your words. No-one likes a rasping and screeching tune; it will mar your message. Now, take a deep breath – literally!

Breath

Try talking while breathing in. It's impossible. We can only talk on an out-breath. Breath is what gives your voice its quality and power. It is key to mastering your nervousness and boosting your confidence. To maximise your vocal resonance, a technique called **diaphragmatic breathing** is best.

The diaphragm is a horizontal muscle that lies below the lungs. As you breathe in, the diaphragm opens so that the air enters the deepest part of your lungs, slightly displacing your internal organs and pushing out your stomach. As you breathe

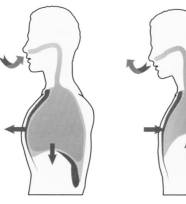
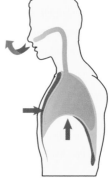

Expanding   Contracting

ILLUSTRATION: Shutterstock

out, your lungs contract and your stomach pulls in. With diaphragmatic breathing there is almost no movement in your chest or shoulders. You breathe like this naturally when you are relaxed or sleeping. (See p89 for more.)

Volume

Above all, you need to be loud enough to be heard. If your audience can't hear you, you may as well stay at home.

A voice that is slightly louder than average conveys confidence and certainty. When people are uncertain about what they want to say, they often drop their voice in the unconscious hope they won't be heard.

But if you constantly speak louder than normal, it will get irritating – and if you get to the point of shouting, you will sound aggressive. What's more, we have all encountered soft-spoken people who convey more authority than loud-mouthed blowhards.

The key is to use a combination of both. If you generally speak with a loud voice, what do you do when you really want to capture your audience's attention? Dropping your voice will draw them in. On the other hand, if you are a soft speaker, raising your voice will. In both cases you're breaking the pattern, and that's what grabs their attention.

Pitch

A deep voice is associated with competence, strength and integrity – voters are more likely to elect leaders with lower-pitched voices.[3] That's unfortunate for men like me with a relatively high-pitched voice, and of course for women, whose voices are on average twice as high as men's. Fortunately, pitch is something we can all work on.

VOICE EXERCISE – A DEEPER PITCH

Take in a deep, diaphragmatic breath and let out a low pitched hum on an 'Ahh' sound for as long as you can. If your lips are properly relaxed, you will feel them gently vibrate. You may also feel vibrations through your head and chest. Repeat several times, each time trying to get your voice lower and lower without straining it.

When we're nervous we generally raise our pitch – think of a voice cracking under pressure – which is one of the other reasons I'll also be sharing some relaxation tools with you. However, constantly speaking at the same pitch, high or low, would become monotonous and bore your audience. As with volume, variety is key. And, no matter your normal pitch, avoid 'upspeak' – when you raise your pitch at the end of your sentences, so that statements sound like questions. This makes you sound uncertain and reduces your credibility.

Pace

We're more inclined to believe people who speak faster than average. This is partly because they seem more certain but also because it's more mentally taxing to assess the validity of the content at a faster pace. Once again, though, variety is key; if you've been speaking at a rapid clip, slowing down will emphasise your point.

Articulation

Speech can only be understood through the articulation of clear and distinct vowels and consonants. We all sound different due to our accents, and there is nothing wrong with an accent – but there *is* something wrong if your vowels and consonants can't be distinguished. This isn't dependent on your mother tongue; there are first-language English speakers who can't be understood because they don't pronounce words properly.

Right or wrong, we associate good articulation with intelligence. More importantly, without it we may not be properly understood.

Pausing

Pausing... is imperative.

When you're speaking, the listener doesn't have the benefit of punctuation. Your pauses chunk the meaning so that what you're saying can be understood. Pauses can be short, medium or long. The longer your pause, the more time you give your audience to reflect on your previous point. If the point was emotional, a pause will deepen the emotion. As you hold off sharing your next piece of information, a pause creates... suspense.

Finally, pauses let your mind catch up to your mouth. When you're searching for a word, the classic mistake is to use hesitating filler sounds, such as 'um', 'ah' and 'er', or filler words, such as 'you know' and 'like'. A pause is far preferable: instead of bumbling and ill-prepared, you will sound authoritative.

FACIAL EXPRESSION

Smile

Smile. This advice may seem obvious, but I've found that pitch presenters tend to smile less than they would normally because they are nervous, or perhaps because they feel they won't be taken seriously. Not true.

A smile is one of the quickest ways to boost positive feelings, both for the one receiving the smile *and* for the one smiling. There is a facial feedback loop in the brain: when we're happy we smile but, equally, when we smile we feel happy.[4] Just looking at a smile is pleasurable. When you smile at someone, even if they try to not smile back, the part of their brain that activates smiling will be triggered.

Amazingly, even a fake smile – one that does not involve the eyes – elevates the mood and reduces heart rate and feelings of nervousness. Frowns have the opposite effect. Of course, a fixed grin could make you come across as an axe murderer!

Keep it real by varying your facial expressions. And bear in mind that any facial expression will have increased impact when it's authentic.

Eye Contact

Think about talking to someone who never looks at you. You'd likely think they were very nervous, they had something to hide or they didn't consider you important.

Eye contact is one of the most powerful ways to create empathy and rapport. Research shows that when two people stare into each other's eyes for even a couple of minutes, without saying a word, their liking for each other increases.[5] A whole raft of studies show how much more persuasive we are when we make eye contact. In one example, people were much more likely to agree to a marketing survey if they were looked in the eye.[6]

So how do you make eye contact with a panel or a larger audience? When you're talking to a larger group you can't constantly make eye contact with each person. But if you focus on individuals, everyone will feel a greater sense of connection and intimacy with you. Avoid talking *at* the room or even sections of the room; pick out one individual over there and talk to them for a few moments, then another over here and do the same.

Some years ago I was in the audience when Bill Clinton gave a presentation. Clinton is renowned as one of the greatest connectors of all time. (Occasionally he connected a little too much!) For a large part of the speech he seemed to be talking directly to me. In an audience of a few thousand people this was impossible; he was simply focusing on specific people. Those in the vicinity of his gaze would have felt he was looking at them, or they would have vicariously felt the intimacy he was creating with whomever he was looking at.

Of course, it's easier to make eye contact with everyone when addressing a smaller group, as in most pitches. But some presenters have a tendency to look only at the key decision-maker, making everyone else feel less important. Others look everywhere *but* at the key decision-maker. In a smaller group, be sure to give everyone the courtesy of your eye contact.

BODY LANGUAGE
Posture and Movement

Before you even open your mouth, how you stand says a whole lot about you. A slouched posture conveys low confidence or disinterest. A relaxed, upright posture conveys confidence and ease. Just as smiling changes the way you feel, so does your posture. Standing in a bold, upright posture will not only raise your confidence but also increase people's perception of your confidence.[7] Aristotle used to tell men going into war: if you don't feel courageous, act courageous and the feeling will follow. I call it changing ourselves from the outside in.

> 'Body language is more powerful than words.'
> – Ricky Gervais

When I first started as a professional speaker, I thought all was going swimmingly until I watched a video of myself. I was pacing up and down like an expectant father waiting for news of his first-born. All that movement would have irritated the audience and distracted them from my message. This is why watching videos of yourself in action is so valuable: you get to see yourself doing things that you simply don't pick up when you're mid-speech.

When you move, it should be for a reason. If you need to emphasise something or shift to a new point, taking a step forward or to the side can give your point additional impact. Just remember that if you generally stand still, any movements you do make will be accentuated.

When you're standing still, keep your weight even but slightly forward. Avoid leaning to one side. Use movement deliberately.

Unless you're pitching one-on-one or the entire pitch is Q&A, you will almost always pitch standing up. While one team member speaks, the others can remain seated. You could sit around a boardroom table with the selection committee, or for a different, informal approach, up ahead on bar stools. The pitch leader should sit in the most central position. While your colleague presents, it's important to focus on them with a positive facial expression and upright posture. This demonstrates liking and interest, which also provides another indication that you are a close-knit team.

Gestures

Movements of the hands and arms can add significant impact to your message. Notice how we sometimes beat our hand up and down on each word of a sentence to emphasise its importance. Or we may raise our hands to make a point or lower them as we draw to a conclusion. These are **beat gestures**, which follow the rhythm of our speech.

By contrast, **iconic gestures** help to illustrate a point. We may rub our shoulders while we talk about being cold, or open our arms wide to demonstrate the size of something.

Research shows that when a word is accompanied by a supportive gesture, it reduces the effort required to understand it.[8] But note, also, that there are hand/arm positions to steer clear of.

Avoid:

- Keeping your arms crossed in front of you;
- Putting your hands in your pockets;
- Holding your hands behind your back or in front of you (where they will do little to contribute to the impact of your message).

That's not to say you have to be constantly gesturing, or that the occasional hand in pocket is a deal-breaker. Also, allowing your arms to hang at your sides some of the time will help amplify the gestures that you do make.

Touch

If you're wondering how effective touch is as a non-verbal form of communication, just imagine someone slapping you across the face or kissing you on the cheek. You'll get the respective messages loud and clear. During your pitch there's no place for touching – and certainly no slapping or kissing! – but during one-on-one communications, before and after, there may be. The kind of touch we're looking for here is light and non-sexual, and usually takes place on the upper arm or shoulder. Touch communicates positive regard and makes people much more agreeable.

> - Restaurant servers who touch patrons lightly on the arm or shoulder get significantly bigger tips.
> - When signature-gatherers asked strangers to sign a petition, 55 percent did so. When they touched people once on the upper arm, the percentage jumped to 81.
> - Car salesmen who lightly touched prospective buyers were rated much more positively than those who didn't. [9]

Why is touch so powerful? We are social creatures. To survive and thrive we depend on our connections to others. We connect in many ways – conversationally, emotionally, commercially. Touch connects us at the most basic level – physically. Touch releases a cascade of feel-good neurochemicals in the brain and lowers cortisol, the stress hormone. The brain rewards us for touching and being touched because it places a high value on social bonding. When you touch someone appropriately you will be associated with these good feelings, making them more open to your message.

Your use of touch should be part of the natural rapport that you are already building. Of course, it must never be overbearing or intrusive. As obvious as this may sound, it needs repeating: touch should be strictly non-sexual. If there is any possibility it could be perceived as sexual or inappropriate, rather err on the side of caution and avoid it.

Even the right kind of touch can be inappropriate. Someone hunched over, with folded arms and a scowl, would probably not welcome a friendly pat on the shoulder. When you do touch, it should usually be combined with other positive non-verbal cues such as eye contact and smiling.

GROOMING

In the 1960 American presidential election, Richard Nixon was widely expected to beat John F Kennedy. He had just finished a successful eight-year run as vice-president to a hugely popular president and war hero, Dwight D Eisenhower. Kennedy was young, inexperienced and Catholic – considered by many at the time to be an unwinnable combination. The debates were supposed to put the nail in the coffin of Kennedy's aspirations. And if you were listening to the first debate on radio that's probably what you would have thought happened. Listeners awarded Nixon a victory. Yet the larger television audience, estimated at a phenomenal 70 million people, thought Kennedy had won. How did that happen, given that the TV and radio audience heard the exact same thing?

They may have *heard* the same thing, but what they saw was very different. Kennedy looked tanned, fit and well rested. Nixon wore an ill-fitting shirt and, having turned down make-up, sweated profusely under the hot lights. Worst of all, his five-o-clock shadow, accentuated on black-and-white TV, made him look shifty.

That first debate ruined Nixon's chances – which is to say, this was probably the first American election won (or lost) because of personal grooming.

Subsequent presidential races have been obsessed with the candidates' grooming, from their hairstyles to the colour of their ties, and with good reason. Nixon himself learnt from his debating debacle. He fared better – though not well enough – in the three subsequent debates with Kennedy, and he was far better prepared for the 1968 presidential race, which he won comfortably.

Good grooming may seem obvious. Shave, brush your hair, wear a good suit. It may also seem like the triumph of style over substance. But don't dismiss it. Grooming is an indicator of health and hygiene. If people are going to work with you, they need to see that you are well, and they deduce that from your external appearance.

Depending on your profession, you may wish to convey a unique impression, with a look that's out of the ordinary. One popular conference speaker presents in shorts, T-shirt and cap turned backwards. The casualness of your attire is less the concern here.

What's most important is that you present yourself in a deliberate way that reflects the image of what you want others to see and think. Whatever your look, make sure you exude the health and wellbeing of a Kennedy rather than the dishevelled weariness of a Nixon.

BENEATH THE SURFACE

THE POWER OF IMPERFECT PRESENCE

A number of years ago I was the closing speaker for a large telecoms company at the Sun City Superbowl, one of the most prestigious venues in Africa. More than a thousand people, including the upper echelon of the company, were in the audience. The conference organiser assured me that if I shone, there would be a lot more work for me. Afterwards, both my client and a key member of the board congratulated me on hitting each one of their key objectives for the session. A week later the client dropped me an email: I had bombed.

At the time, neither she nor I had realised it; on the contrary, we thought I'd done well. But my audience rating was a six out of ten. In the speaking business that's the guillotine. Comments ranged from the bad – 'didn't connect' – to the ugly – 'irrelevant'.

I couldn't understand it. I had customised my presentation to incorporate the company's history and culture, rehearsed my words to perfection – shooting them out with the force of gunfire – dropped my voice to a bass note of authority and made sure my posture was worthy of the Oval Office. And then it started to dawn. My dominance and confidence had alienated them.

The business was going through a painful restructure at the time, with many staff in the process of being retrenched. My powerful communication made them feel less powerful and more resentful. I had executed the perfect presentation – for the wrong audience.

According to Wharton Business School professor Adam Grant, **powerful communication** is when we raise our voices, express certainty and project confidence. We display strength by spreading our arms in dominant poses, commanding as much physical space as possible.[10] Grant calls the alternative **powerless communication**. Here speakers reveal their vulnerability, use self-deprecating humour, disclaimers and even hesitations. He tells the story of a trial lawyer with a stutter who won against far slicker opponents. Jurors commented on how genuine he was. Deep down we're all vulnerable. By revealing our vulnerability, we enable others to empathise with us, making us more human and approachable.

Of course 'powerless communication' is really very powerful. So I prefer the terms **humble communication** versus **confident communication**, and here's a key point: you can project both at the same time. With my telecoms audience I could have still projected my voice boldly, but while doing so

I could have revealed some tough times that I had been through. Or, while providing some guidelines to deal with those tough times, my voice could have been a little gentler and less domineering.

Humble communication is not just appropriate for low-power audiences like my telecoms company. High-powered audiences may also bristle at a domineering communication style because it could threaten their egos. As Grant points out, however, expressing vulnerability is only effective when the audience is convinced of the speaker's competence; if they're not, it only reinforces the perception of incompetence. The ideal is to come across as down to earth and an expert at the same time.

When we are pitching, we are selling. In one study, people ranked 'salesperson' as the second-least most socially responsible occupation, barely above stock broker.[11] No wonder that in conventional, pushy sales mode we will often be perceived as less likeable and trustworthy. By revealing some vulnerability, we can counteract this impression and increase trust.

I once worked with a pitching client who had a slight speech defect. English wasn't his first language and he pronounced 'th' as 'f'. It was a couple of days before the pitch and I thought I could help him correct the error. Instead he got more and more frustrated, and I had to work hard to rebuild his confidence. In retrospect I should have left it. The defect did not prevent anyone

'Showing weakness reveals vulnerability. Revealing vulnerability shows strength.'

from understanding him, and probably added to his approachability. So if you stutter, don't have the deepest voice or most commanding presence, just aim to be competent and genuine; your imperfections could give you an advantage.

ADAPTABILITY

Clearly it is neither necessary nor advisable to change every aspect of our presence in some mythical pursuit of perfection. But sometimes people I advise tell me that making even subtle changes to their non-verbal communication feels artificial.

It's worthwhile remembering that the word 'artificial' means to skilfully create. There is nothing wrong with skilfully creating your presence. You didn't come out of the womb presenting yourself in the way that you do today; you learned those behaviours unconsciously. There is no reason not to learn better ones.

I was a shy child who seldom made eye contact. Even as an adult, when I first started public speaking I found it difficult to make eye contact with the audience. If I was to go with my 'natural' way, I still wouldn't. Instead, understanding the importance of eye contact, I made the effort to change, and now eye contact has become second nature for me.

In general, adaptability is key to improvement. But we also need to be adaptable within the pitch. When I coach a team, we spend a long time crafting a compelling story (which we'll get to). The opening story is often a highly emotive attention grabber. On one pitch I worked on, within thirty seconds of his story, the team leader was interrupted by the CEO with a question. Even though the team had been told to prepare an opening speech, this CEO had changed his mind (exhibiting some adaptability of his own!). Perhaps his reaction was designed to see how adaptable the team was, or perhaps he was just impatient. While it was a surprise, we had prepared for this possibility and the leader was able to switch to a discussion seamlessly, with the team embedding some of their story and talking points into their answers.

> **'The measure of intelligence is the ability to change.'**
> – Albert Einstein

BIG PITCH TEMPERAMENT

Many people rate the fear of public speaking as greater than the fear of death.[12] That means most people would rather be in the casket than giving the eulogy! How do you ensure that on show day your nerves don't get the better of you? The power of your presence depends on your being able to control your nerves. If you can't, you're going to lose your confidence and the ability to deliver your message.

The Stress Response

The scientific term for nervousness is the stress response. Understanding it will help you control it.

First things first: stress is not the enemy. Stress is the arousal that enables us to stay awake and active. Too little stress/arousal and you'd be asleep before standing up to give your presentation. But too much and you reduce your ability to think clearly.

Pioneering stress researchers Yerkes and Dodson developed a helpful graph to understand the relationship between stress and performance. Notice how up to a point stress increases performance – but beyond that point, as stress levels rise, performance decreases.

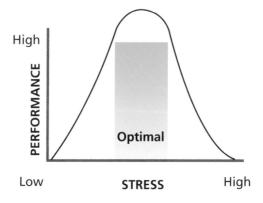

Performance-enhancing stress is known as eustress. Performance-decreasing stress is known as distress. But even distress has its place; in fact, without it we wouldn't be here.

Distress

We are the descendants of cavemen who were in continual threat of being eaten by a hungry tiger or an angry uncle. The ones who survived long enough to mate needed to be able to do one of two things really well: fight or flight. In today's world there may be no sabre-toothed tiger, just a sabre-toothed client. No death threat, just a deadline. Yet the body responds to an emotional threat as if it were a physical threat: the 'fight or flight' instinct kicks in. Breathing, blood pressure and heart rate speed up to get blood to the muscles, where it's needed for fight or flight. When you're feeling distressed your body is readying for a life-or-death battle.

Why do so many people become distressed when they have to give a speech? People are the most social creatures on the planet. We depend on our fellow human beings to survive and thrive. For our caveman ancestors, being rejected from the tribe would almost certainly mean death. To the primitive part of your brain, standing alone in front of a group of people to give a speech can feel like you're facing that primitive horde. Soon they will decide whether to accept or reject you. No wonder the stress hormones start pumping.

The good news is that we have another part of our brains that can put on the stress brakes.

Two Brains

The brain is enormously complex, but for our purposes it's helpful to think of ourselves as having two brains. The primitive brain sits lower down in the head. Known as the reptilian brain, this is the part of the brain that to some degree we share with – you guessed it – reptiles. It was the earliest part of the brain to evolve and it focuses on threat detection and survival.

Higher up, in the front of our head, we have our prefrontal neocortex. This is the most evolved part of the brain where we have language, executive function and self-control.

When we're very stressed, the blood, glucose and nutrients shift away from the prefrontal cortex to the reptilian brain. That's why high levels of stress reduce our ability to think clearly, and we are more likely to lose our temper and do something we regret. Afterwards, we may even say, 'I lost it.' It's true: we lost our higher brain.

There are two effective ways to re-engage your higher brain and destress. You can do it physically or mentally.

BODY OVER MIND
Exercise

Remember, high levels of stress are preparing you for a massive physical response: fight or flight. That's why one of the best treatments for stress is physical exercise. When you move your body vigorously, the stress hormones are absorbed from your blood into your muscles, effectively giving you a substitute for fight or flight. I almost always exercise on the day I'm giving a presentation. Not only do I find myself calmer, but my oxygenated brain also comes up with better ideas more rapidly.

Breathe

Stress response breathing tends to be shallow breathing that expands the chest and raises the shoulders. This is good if you're trying to get short, sharp shots of oxygen to run from a lion. Not so much if you want to give a relaxed speech.

By contrast, **relaxation response breathing** is slow, deep, rhythmic breathing. When we slow our breathing, we lower our heart rate and blood pressure, reducing the stress response. We also shift blood, glucose and nutrients from the lower to higher brain, improving our clarity of thought.

JUST BREATHE

The most effective breathing technique I know to induce the relaxation response is what I call *two-four, slow, deep belly breathing*, which gets the air into the deepest part of your lungs.

Put your hand on your tummy. Breathe in on the count of two. As you breathe in your tummy will slightly expand. Now breathe out on the count of four. As you breathe out your tummy goes in. This you may recall is *diaphragmatic breathing*, which also boosts your vocal quality. The diaphragm is a horizontal muscle that lies below the lungs. The reason your tummy

---

expands when you breathe in is because your inflated lungs are slightly pushing out your internal organs. When you breathe out your lungs contract, pulling in your tummy.

Why double the time of the out-breath? Well, if you breathe in you'll notice that you actually feel slightly more stressed. Breathe out and you'll find yourself feeling more relaxed. There is in fact a slight stress response associated with an in-breath and a slight relaxation response on an out-breath. By extending the out-breath we naturally prolong the relaxation response.

The way we talk to ourselves also determines our stress levels. So instead of just breathing out on the count of four, rather breathe out while internally saying the word 'calm' to four beats: 'Ca – ah – ah – alm'. This is a subtle form of self-hypnosis where you are further programming your brain into a state of relaxation.

MIND OVER MATTER

Physical exercise and breathing exercises are useful if you're feeling highly stressed in the days leading up to a pitch. However, trying to relax just before a nerve-wracking pitch can, ironically, *increase stress* in the immediate term, because it takes effort to overcome our natural state. At this point it's better to use one of two mental processes, the **reappraisal** and **acceptance** techniques.

Reappraisal

When scientists measure stress they will often get people to – no surprises – give a speech. To make sure the stress hormones flow abundantly, research subjects may be asked to speak about their weaknesses to a panel of experts who sigh irritably and roll their eyes. Sadism is a useful trait in stress researchers! Unsurprisingly, for most people the stress response kicks in.

In one study, researchers got participants to flip their script. Before giving their speech, they were told that the stress they were going to feel was actually good. Their increased breathing was pumping oxygen into their brains, making them more alert. Their rapid heartbeat was helping them raise their performance. Their bodies were gearing them not for fear and failure but courage and success. Nervousness and excitement share a similar underlying physiology. The researchers were helping them shift the one into the other by changing their interpretation of their experience. Amazingly, those who were taught to see their stress response as positive were not just less anxious, their hearts pumped more efficiently and their blood vessels didn't constrict.[14] Vascular constriction is what makes stress dangerous.

How you let your higher brain talk to you has a major impact on how stressed you feel. So if you're feeling nervous before going into a pitch, reframe your nervousness as excitement. Tell yourself you're *excited* to get out there, and pitch to win!

Acceptance

There is one more mental technique that may help you, particularly if you find it challenging to reinterpret the physical symptoms of stress: *acceptance*. Simply accepting your sensations of stress, and even the negative thoughts that may arise, reduces the additional stress that comes when you tell yourself you shouldn't be feeling nervous. That doesn't mean you're agreeing with the negative thoughts. Rather, you accept that they are just brain events. You don't have to react to them; they will pass of their own accord and possibly quicker if you just let them be.

If you notice an uncomfortable sensation or a negative thought, instead of trying to change it, simply acknowledge it by saying, 'There is a sensation,' or, 'There is a thought.'

HABITS

Any new behaviour requires conscious application at first. Think about the way you first started driving a car. You had to expend large amounts of energy to coordinate all the movements required to accelerate, brake and steer. Indicating was for professionals! Now you do all that largely unconsciously. Driving has become a habit. Slowing down your breathing, making eye contact, lifting your posture or speaking in a more resonant, deeper tone takes time to become habitual. Initially you will need to do it with conscious deliberation.

> 'We are what we repeatedly do. Excellence, then, is not an act but a habit.'
> – Aristotle

Estimates vary, but it can take anywhere from a few days to a few months for a new behaviour to become a habit.[15] If it feels artificial at first, just remember: the more you do it, the more natural it will begin to feel.

Don't just rehearse the words, rehearse your presence.

TUNE IN
TEAM
OPTIMISM
PRESENCE
PURPOSE
S

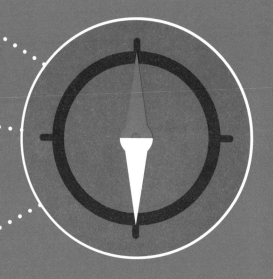

CHAPTER 5

PURPOSE

'It's not about you. It's about what you can do for them.'

Many years ago, when I was trying to sell my first book and I finally managed to get a major publisher on the line, I found that I was a little nervous. Okay, I was *very* nervous. Sweaty palms, dry mouth, heart racing. Stumbling my way through my phone pitch, I heard a click. She'd put the phone down. I was mortified. I felt like such a fool.

Back then, if you told me that in time I would be considered one of the world's leading experts on pitching for business, I would have said you were smoking something. Forget selling my book to a publisher, I couldn't pitch half-price crack to a crack addict – which is good because that would have got us both arrested. You get my point.

When I thought of sales I thought of some obnoxious guy pushing something that no-one wanted. Then I discovered something that totally transformed my view of selling. My friend Bob Burg shared with me what the word 'sell' really means. I love etymology, the origins of words. If you really want to understand a word, go to its origins. The word sell come from the Old English *sellan*, which meant 'to give'.

That was my light-bulb moment. I had been confusing selling with *taking*. If you don't like the idea of selling it's probably because you're making the same mistake I made. If you're a good person, you don't want to be a taker. As long as I thought of selling as taking I just couldn't sell. When I approached selling as *giving*, my results exploded. Flipping my internal script from taker to giver flipped my results into the stratosphere.

SERVICE BEFORE SELF

Great salespeople are givers. They give great value; they give of themselves. And they often give before they get. They prove their value by giving high-value information, product samples or, more important than all of that, their ear. Great salespeople are great *listeners*. They help people figure out what they really need and want. That's why the first key to a winning pitch is Tune In!

The best salespeople are there to serve. And service is spiritual. That's right, selling – great selling – is spiritual! Of course, at the end of it all, selling is also taking. We give value and *take* money. (That's good – people generally place greater value on what they pay for.) But if you're primarily a giver and selling makes you feel like a taker, your brain will sabotage you and you won't be good at pitching.

So how do you get into a giver's mindset? Before you go into pitch, one question you can ask yourself to activate your purpose is:

'How are these people going to be better off because of me?'

Most people going in to a pitch focus on how they're going to be better off by winning. Better than focusing on what you're going to *take,* focus on what you're going to *give.* (I guess this book could be called *Pitch To Serve!*)

In a Wharton Business School study, one group of salespeople read stories about customers who had benefited from the services of the company. Think of these salespeople as the *purpose group*, focusing on 'how we make a difference in the world'. The second group read stories about people in the same job who had increased their skills. Let's call them the *personal benefit* group, focusing on 'what's in it for me'. Both groups then went out to sell. Incredibly, the purpose group achieved *double* the sales of the personal benefit group. [1]

The difference between a purpose-driven approach and a personal-benefit approach is the difference between a missionary and a mercenary.

Mercenaries are totally in it for themselves; missionaries are there to serve. This research proves that we can all be either; it just

'The purpose of life is to live a life of purpose.'

– Robert Byrne

depends on our mindset. Ironically, when you're a missionary you're better able to serve your own self-interest in the long run.

Purpose doesn't just boost your influence, it boosts your resilience. Quoting Friedrich Nietzsche, the holocaust survivor Viktor Frankl said, **'He who has a Why to live can bear almost any How.' When you have a compelling reason, a deep purpose, you will do what you need to achieve your goal.**

A Carnegie Mellon University study found that thinking about their life purpose before a test increased students' problem-solving ability by 50 percent, most likely by reducing stress levels. When you're purpose-driven, not only does it reduce your stress, it boosts your performance. Make sure you remind yourself of your purpose before you go into your pitch.

The most inspiring company I've ever had the privilege to work with is 'budget store' PEP. Eighteen years ago, they were nearly bankrupt. Today they're the biggest single-brand retailer in Africa, and they've achieved double-digit growth in that time. How did they do it? They got clear about their purpose.

Eighteen years ago, if you asked a senior manager at PEP what they did, they would have said something like, 'We provide apparel for LSM 3-6.' Today, ask them what they do and they'll tell you, 'We serve remarkable people who have to get by on a very small budget so that they and their families can live with dignity and pride.' Period.

Once they got clear about their mission they were able to provide school uniforms at a price that no-one else can, but of the quality of much higher-priced products. You can't give people cheap things that fall apart and serve their pride. Their former MD Leon Lourens liked to say, 'A company that only exists to make money is a very poor company indeed.' PEP has become a very rich company by focusing on purpose.

Just ask yourself who you would choose: someone who was only in it for themselves or someone who was driven by a deep purpose to serve you?

THE ELEVATOR PITCH

If you were in an elevator with your perfect prospect and you had just 20 seconds to describe what you do, what would you say? Most people would say what they do. 'Hi, I'm am accountant/author/security expert.' That's why most people are quickly forgotten. Instead of saying what you can do, say *what you can do for them*.

Imagine you were in a lift with a stranger. You ask him what he does and he says, 'We've developed this really amazing accommodation booking app.' You'd probably be praying the lift was a fast one.

But what if he answered, 'We enable you to book rooms with locals rather than hotels.' If nothing else you would be intrigued to know more. That means you would probably ask a question that leads to a conversation that carries on beyond the opening of that elevator door.

That's the way now-billionaire Brian Chesky pitched Airbnb to investors. They were intrigued enough to help turn his idea into the biggest accommodation company in the world. Chesky treated his pitch as a purpose statement. He realised that people care less about the app and more about what it can do for them.

Now, if you want, you can combine the two. Chesky could have said, 'We have an app that enables you to book rooms with locals rather than hotels.' Just don't emphasise the product. Emphasise its value.

What I love about a good elevator pitch is it forces you to clarify your purpose, and then pitch it!

DOING THE RIGHT THING

The pitch is a promise. You can win a pitch with a lie – once. The tools I'm sharing with you have no moral compass. A sage or charlatan may use them, but the charlatan is soon found out. Let's never forget, we're not pitching to win a job, we're pitching to win a long-term relationship, and that's built on trust.

Like sport, pitching is a high-stakes competition where the incentive to cheat is high. Few people will pitch a bald-faced lie but the obsession with winning can lead to a whiff of inauthenticity that reduces the chances of winning. Think of the stereotypical used-car sales-man. He's slick and he knows his stuff, but you sense he's just telling you what you want to hear so he can make a buck.

> 'Character may almost be called the most effective form of persuasion.'
> – Aristotle

There's nothing wrong with wanting the deal – that desire is why you're reading this book. But we need to remember *why* we want the deal. It's about more than making a buck. What we're really pitching is our purpose, our reason for being. When you're clear about that you're more likely to convey your sincerity and build trust. You're also more likely to do the right thing. We're more likely to win when we focus on serving, rather than winning.

PURPOSE IN THE PROJECT

I worked with an auditing firm that was pitching for the business of a bank. Both the firm and the bank had a focus on contributing to the success of the African continent. Africa, with all its challenges and opportunities, became central to the pitch. This turned the team into missionaries, reminding them that more than making a sale they were partnering with like-minded people to build the continent. There are few reasons more compelling to a partner than an alignment of purpose. More than a guiding ethos, the purpose becomes the core theme on which the pitch is built.

Similarly, Professor Adam Grant tells the story of a French firm headquartered in a small town in the middle of France that had a much-loved soccer team. The firm was being pressured to move to a big city. This would destroy jobs in the small town. The executives felt a responsibility to the town, but to remain they would need a major reorganisation.

They issued a request for proposals for a consultancy to handle the restructure. But it was clear that there was one consultancy they would not work with – the one that had been working with their chief competitor. The firm worried that inside information could be leaked and, as a result, all previous proposals from this consultancy had been rejected. Undaunted by rejection, the consultancy tried once more. During this pitch, the firm once again made it clear that, while they liked the proposal, they couldn't trust that their interests would be placed first. At that point in the pitch each consultant pulled out a blue scarf of the city's beloved soccer team and put it over their shoulders. The lead partner explained that he lived down the road from their headquarters, and that he and his team were equally determined to see the town continue to flourish.

Finally, the firm could see that they had a shared purpose. The consultancy won the job.[2]

Pulling out a scarf to demonstrate you're fans of the same football team may seem gimmicky, but under the circumstances it demonstrated a shared commitment to the survival of this town. Besides, what seems like a superficial similarity can have a profound impact on behaviour.

Just consider this. When Manchester United soccer fans saw a runner slip on the grass, grab his ankle and scream in pain just a third of them stopped to help. However, if the injured runner was wearing a Man-U T-shirt, 92 percent helped. Manchester United fans are very nice people as long as you're a Manchester United fan! Why? Because fans share a purpose.

We like people who are like us. One of the most cherished parts of ourselves is our purpose. If your prospective clients believe you share the same mission, they will believe you are alike in the most fundamental of ways. The third reason why top European companies chose a winning pitch was cultural fit. At the heart of culture is purpose.

TUNE IN
TEAM
OPTIMISM
PRESENCE
PURPOSE
STORY

CHAPTER 6

S TORY

'The best story wins.'

While I was still developing the Pitch To Win programme, I was invited to present my keynote presentation 'What's Your Story?' at the IBM Global Entrepreneur of the Year awards in Cape Town. The winner of the African leg of the contest was the Kenyan telecoms startup Mode, the company I briefly introduced at the beginning of the book.

IBM then asked me to help Mode work on their pitch for the later rounds of the competition, specifically to create and tell the story of their business. After my time with them, Mode went on to win not only the semifinals in Brazil, but also the finals in New York, beating top startups from all over the world. They were kind enough to give the Pitch To Win method some of the credit for their success.

PHOTO: COURTESY IBM

Michael Bloomberg, then mayor of New York, congratulates Julian Kyulu and Josphat Kinyua of Mode, winner of IBM Global Entrepreneur of the Year.

THE POWER OF STORY

Like many entrepreneurs starting new businesses, the guys at Mode had a great idea; they just didn't have a great story.

In my book *The Astonishing Power Of Story* I distinguish between two kinds of stories: **dead stories** and **living stories**. Dead stories are dry and abstract. They provide facts but they don't connect those facts to specific people or situations, and so they tend to be emotionless and boring. As the perfect example, here is the copy from Mode's original presentation:

> Mode is a Kenyan telecoms startup led by CEO Julian Kyula, COO Josphat Kinyua, Chairman Chris Baxter and Director Adel Kambar. Our clients include MTN, Airtel and Glo. Our service is available in 15 countries around the world. We enable telecoms clients to get microcredit through their cellphone provider. This means if someone has run out of call time, using their cellphone they can immediately get credit to top up. Using the same system we eventually hope to provide them with credit that can be used to pay for other things too, like water and electricity.

You may not realise what a brilliant idea this is. But take a look when it's reframed using the living story that they told to win the competition.

Only 26 percent of the world's population have access to bank loans, yet 85 percent of people have a cellphone. Not being able to get credit not only depresses an economy, it really depressed my mother-in-law. She's a florist. Like many people in the developing world she often runs out of cellphone call time, making it impossible for her to call the market to find out if they have the flowers she needs. It's not unusual for her to get a taxi all the way to the market only to find that the flowers haven't arrived, wasting money she could have used to grow her business. With Mode she can now top up her call time with microcredit using her cellphone. Not only does she save money and time, best of all, I have a happy mother-in-law! Soon we'll be rolling out credit for other things like water and electricity. Mode turns your cellphone into a financial lifeline, providing the world's unbanked with nano-credit in a nano-second.

Notice that in the living story there are still facts, and two critical statistics: the ratio of people who have bank accounts to those who have cellphones. But the story gives life to those numbers. It demonstrates exactly how this product can improve the lives of all those people who don't have bank accounts. It answers the single most important question of any presentation: *why?* Nobody ever invested in a business without a very good reason. Telling us *what* the business is and *how* it works does not answer *why* it should exist. Relating a story of the impact your product or service has on a customer's life answers that question.

The final sentence summarises the unique selling proposition using a metaphor – 'turning your cellphone into a financial lifeline… providing nano-credit in a nano-second'. I call a metaphorical catchphrase like this an **instant story**. In a few words you capture the key idea in a rich, emotive image. (We'll learn how to create these later.)

FACTS WITH A HEART

People sometimes resist stories because they don't seem sufficiently factual. But stories *are* facts; they're just facts with a heart.

Stalin is reputed to have said, 'One death is a tragedy, one million is a statistic.' It's cold but true. We can't feel for a number. We *can* feel for a flesh and blood person like ourselves. If we don't feel, we generally don't act. People move emotionally before they move any other way.

'Stories are data with a soul.'
– Brené Brown

When Mode CEO Julian Kyula told the story of his mother-in-law at the IBM Entrepreneur of the Year award finale, he made it personal. Not only did the judges and investors get to connect with his customer's pain and see how his service was easing that pain, they got to connect with him. Clearly Julian wanted to do more than just make money; he had personal experience that had motivated him to dream up this brilliant business.

People invest in you even more than in your idea. When you can connect yourself to the story, you help them get to know and like you.

THE SCIENCE OF STORY

To understand just why stories are so powerful we need to understand one of the most important discoveries in brain science.

It's a hot summer's day in 1995 at the University of Parma, Italy. A monkey is sitting with electrodes attached to its brain, so that researchers can assess the brain's response to movement. Whenever the monkey picks up a peanut to eat, certain neurons fire in its brain and the machine goes brrp brrp.

At lunch time a student walks into the laboratory with an ice cream. The monkey stares at him and then something astonishing happens: as the man raises the cone to his lips – brrp, brrp – the machine goes off. Even though it is sitting completely still, just watching the student lift the cone to his lips makes the monkey's brain respond as if the animal is making the movement himself. Called *mirror neurons*, these microscopic brain cells fire both when we observe an action and when we act ourselves. I say 'we' because it was soon discovered that humans have an even more sophisticated network of mirror neurons covering several parts of the brain.

When you watch somebody walking, for instance, part of your brain – your mirror neuron network – simulates the action as if it is you doing the walking. (Note: you won't actually get a workout this way!)

This understanding began a modern revolution in brain science. Up to this point, it had been thought that the brain was like a window through which we looked at the world. Now we know the brain is more of a virtual-reality machine. To understand what other people are doing, we don't just observe – we experience it internally as if we are doing it ourselves.

As we discovered earlier, we mirror the emotions and behaviour of the people around us. As the presenter of a pitch, your audience will focus their attention on you, leading them to mirror your emotional state. That's why your passion and confidence are so important.

Mirror neurons also explain the power of stories. With our mirror neurons we don't just listen to the story, we live it. Have you noticed that when you're watching a good film or reading a book, you become the hero? That's your mirror neurons giving you the experience of being there yourself.

If you are a consultant, you might tell me that your company has an extensive network of relationships that you will draw on to solve my problems. Sure. That makes sense. But far better to tell me a story about a client who was faced with a multimillion-dollar tax liability, and how you leveraged one of your key connections to identify a legitimate loophole that

'Your emotions are contagious – infect the world with enthusiasm!'

cut the bill in half. As you tell me that story I would, thanks to the mirror neurons, find myself walking in that client's shoes, vicariously receiving all the benefits you've bestowed on him.

Stories provide a virtual-reality simulation. Having experienced the benefits virtually, your client is going to want to experience them in reality. This is partly how stories trigger three key drivers of persuasion.

1 Sampling. Have you noticed that when you go into a supermarket there is often a promoter offering you a sample of a new food or drink? Marketers know that one of the best ways of getting us to buy is by getting us to experience the product. If the experience is positive we're going to want more of it. The likelihood of a purchase after receiving a sample can increase by as much as 90 percent.[1] Stories give your prospects a virtual sample. By walking in the shoes of someone who has had a successful experience with your services, I feel as if I have had a similar experience myself, and I now want the real thing.

2 **Social proof.** Why did those memorable 1980s toothpaste ads tell us that more than 80 percent of dentists used Colgate? Because to save energy we use heuristics – mental short cuts. Following what other people are doing is one of the quickest and easiest short cuts to figuring out what to do. In fact, more than 80 percent of new buying decisions are made after hearing a story from a satisfied customer.[2] When you tell me a story about a success that you achieved with another client, unconsciously I conclude that if it works for them it will probably work for me.

3 **Avoiding the Reactance Effect.** Have you noticed that there are three ways to get something done? 1) Do it yourself. 2) Pay someone to do it. 3) Forbid your teenagers to do it! Well, there is a teenager inside every one of us. Reactance is the resistance to overt persuasion. This is why hard selling usually doesn't work. No-one wants to feel strong-armed into a sale. To avoid reactance we need to feel that we're making a decision because we *want* to. Tell me to buy, and I may choose to do the opposite to assert my free will. Tell me a story about someone else who bought and benefited, and I make the decision myself.

Memory and Emotion

'People will forget what you said, people will forget what you did, but people will never forget how you made them feel.'

When the American poet Maya Angelou said those words she was touching on a neurological fact – numerous studies show that we are far more likely to remember emotional information than neutral information. This is because, to survive and thrive, humans need to quickly learn what is safe and pleasurable versus what is dangerous and painful. If you were quick to forget that putting your hand in the fire would burn you, you would constantly be getting burnt.

Emotion is the way we register pain and pleasure. Generally, the greater the emotion, the more likely it has survival value and should be remembered. Of course the emotion generated in a story doesn't have a direct impact on our survival, but remember that stories are virtual-reality machines, so our brains respond to them as if they were real life. The higher the emotion you generate in your audience, the more likely they are to remember you and your message.

Good stories also generate suspense, which boosts the brain chemical dopamine. Dopamine happens to improve memory. No wonder that a

Stanford University study found that after listening to speeches, more than 60 percent of students remembered the stories, but just 5 percent remembered the statistics.[3]

HOW STORIES SELL PRODUCTS

To drive home the power of a living story, here is an example from the private healthcare industry, an essential service in countries with poor public healthcare, like my home country South Africa. First, the dead story:

> It is very important that young people have good private healthcare to cover any hospital expenses that may arise. An illness may be unexpected, and if one doesn't have sufficient funds available, one may be faced with both medical and financial problems. Therefore buy a good private healthcare plan.

Now here is the same message as a living story:

> My friend Howard was fit, active and just 24 years old when his doctor told him, 'You've got cancer.' He shook his head in disbelief not realising it was about to get worse. 'We need to get you into a good

private hospital immediately,' said his doctor. 'Do you have a private healthcare plan?' That's when Howard put his head in his hands and started crying. As a young, healthy guy he'd just never seen the point of having private healthcare. Fortunately, after many months of treatment he got better, but to pay his medical costs he had to sell his apartment. Four years later he's still living with his parents. The leading cause of personal bankruptcy is medical crisis.

Which of those two stories is more likely to motivate someone to get private healthcare? Without a doubt the second one. Notice that living stories don't tell us what to think or do. They take us on a journey in someone else's shoes. They give us an experience, after which they allow us to draw our own conclusions. This is what enables them to overcome the reactance effect.

What's the best-selling book of all time? It's called the Bible and it's a collection of lessons dressed up in stories. Our ancestors understood better than us that information is much more likely to stick when it's part of a narrative.

STORY CREATION

THE A.R.T. OF STORYTELLING

Telling stories is like wearing clothes: everyone does it, but some just do it better than others. Simply telling a story does not ensure better communication. It would be better not to tell a story than to tell a long and boring story that doesn't make a relevant point. But even if you don't fancy yourself a storyteller, there is a simple formula that anyone can use to get a story right. The ART story-creation method provides a simple three-step method to ensure that your stories pack a persuasive punch.

T – Take-home Point

With persuasion stories you begin with the end in mind, hence we begin (and then end) with the T. Once you know what information you have to cover, ask yourself what the one thing is that you want your prospective clients to know above all else. Let's say the point is: *when shifting their business to you, the transition will be easy and seamless.*

The take-home point usually expresses a key *benefit* that they will get out of doing business with you. Once you know the point you want to make, start looking for real-life examples that demonstrate it. Think about other people or organisations you've worked with who have received this benefit by adopting your offering, or those who lost out because they never had your offering.

A – Adversity

Every good story, be it a Hollywood movie, a literary novel or an anecdote told in a pitch, involves adversity. A story is not a worthy story without struggle. Something needs to get in the way of our characters achieving what they want. In business terms, adversity is the *problem*. If there were no problem, there would be no pitch. In essence, the pitch is your opportunity to show how you're going to solve their problem. People are about twice as motivated to remove pain than to get pleasure, so if you gloss over the problem you reduce their motivation to take action. Remember: sell to the pain!

'Nothing great happens without overcoming adversity.'

You could share a story of a client who had a negative experience with transition and was reluctant to go through transition again, but when they did finally do so with you, the experience was so seamless that their final comment was 'transition, what transition?'

If you can't find a real example of a negative experience, consider creating a hypothetical example illustrating what *could* go wrong. Without being melodramatic, try to accentuate the adversity wherever possible. Once they are clear about the problem, they need to link you to the solution.

R – Resolution

At this point you need to convey how you resolved the problem. What was your *solution?* How did you overcome the adversity? This is what demonstrates your services and makes people want to buy.

Here is a translation of the ART storytelling method into business.

STORY	Adversity	Resolution	Take home point
BUSINESS	Problem	Solution	Benefit

THE NUTS AND BOLTS

Here are a few extra pointers to bear in mind as you create your stories.

1 Setup

It's usually best to start off the story by introducing the main character or setting up the time or location. 'It was 2.30 in the morning when I got the call...' This eases the audience in, getting them into a receptive, story-listening mode.

2 Detail

Detail adds authenticity, increasing the sense that the story actually took place, and lending you and your offering more credibility. By giving us a sense of what the characters and environment look and feel like, you immerse us in the world of the story. 'Jack was a large, gruff guy, not the sort of person to take what I was going to tell him lightly,' you might say.

One of the theories about why stories are so persuasive is that they create a mild hypnotic trance. As your mind is consumed by the story, you let go of your usual defences: rationality and scepticism. We don't have time for too much detail and you shouldn't be trying to be a literary novelist, but the trance state depends on us being able to picture the events. Of course, the details need to be true; if you come across as a fabricator, the whole process is ruined.

3 Dialogue

Compare the following two versions of the same point.

'While their biggest concern about transition was disruption, by the end they were very happy with the way things went.'

Versus:

'While their biggest concern about transition was disruption, afterwards, when we asked committee chairman Daniel Davis about the transition, he said, 'Transition, what transition?''

Sharing the exact words that someone used increases authenticity and impact. Try to use real-life dialogue where possible. Making up good dialogue is a genuine art – rather just use the real stuff if you can.

THE OPENING STORY

If it's going to be a long pitch – over 20 minutes – it would be good to open with a story of any personal connection you might have to the company. Do you or your family personally love and use their products and services? Think of examples of how this company has touched your life or fulfilled their purpose by solving problems for you or your loved ones?

This is a powerful way to create rapport right at the start, but it needs to be genuine.

STORY PERSPECTIVE

We can tell stories from one of three perspectives: first-person, second-person and third-person. It's worth consciously deciding which to use.

■ **First-person stories.** These are 'I' or 'we' stories told from your perspective, which generally have to do with something that happened to you. Because you're revealing something personal, first-person stories can create a strong empathetic connection to you, the storyteller. This builds rapport with your prospect, which is a key part of what will win you the pitch. First-person stories are also the easiest to tell because all you really need to do is draw on your own memory of the event.

There are two potential problems with this perspective. First, you may not have a story involving you. And second, you need to ensure that you don't just come across as self-aggrandising.

- **Second-person stories.** These are hypothetical scenarios that place the person you're talking to into the story. You might say, 'Imagine you're at your desk, trying to get your work done, trying to bring in business – but you just can't get through it because there are too many complaints. You could cut down your customer complaints in half just by installing our system. You wouldn't have to increase your budget or staff. How would that enable you to grow your business?'

  Second-person stories use the pronoun 'you', which can be very powerful when trying to convince someone of something, because they can actually see themselves getting the benefit of using your products or services. The other term for this is 'future pacing'. You're putting them in the future, enabling them to experience in virtual reality how much better life would be with your service or product.

The one drawback of second-person stories is that they can be seen as a little presumptuous, but if you tuned in properly at the start, and the story speaks directly to the buyer's needs, it should work.

- **Third-person stories.** These are 'he', 'she' or 'they' stories told about someone else. Though it won't feel as personal, your story doesn't have to involve you. I do a lot of work with salespeople who share one another's stories – by doing so they have a far larger pool of stories to choose from to demonstrate the power of their product or service. Telling the story from the perspective of a customer is also a third-person story.

THE OTHER ELEMENTS

THE OPENER

The opening of a presentation is like the first bite of a slice of cake. If the initial taste puts off the diners, they're unlikely to enjoy the rest. And while living stories are the heart and soul of the Pitch To Win formula, there are three other options.

The Shocking Statement

A shocking or surprising statement grabs attention by challenging conventional wisdom. Imagine you're an auditor and you opened your pitch with this:

> 'Within the next ten years, 30 percent of corporate audits will be performed by artificial intelligence. That's according to Klaus Schwab, the founder of the World Economic Forum.' [4]

This approach grabs the attention because it's hardly what you'd expect an auditor to say. It's quick and punchy, and you can now transition into a story showing how much more than an audit your team provides, or even how you're at the forefront of developing that artificial intelligence.

The Powerful Question

Questions tap into our insatiable curiosity to make sense of the world. In a presentation that I do on leadership, I open with: 'Are leaders born or made?'

By pausing after that question, I get the audience reflecting on the answer. I've captured their attention and they're waiting for me to satisfy their curiosity.

> **Questions awaken attention;**
> **answers put attention to bed.**

This is what makes questions great rhetorical devices to use throughout your presentation.

The Personalised Opening

This is a slightly riskier option, which uses something that has just happened to create your opening on the spot. For instance, let's say you just had a cup of tea and you spilled some of it. You could try to kick things off with a little humour, saying, 'I want to start by thanking you for the tea which really has improved the look of my tie.' A well-executed personalised opening tells your audience that this isn't going to be another stock presentation, that you can think on your feet and that you're going to make it special for them.

As an international conference speaker, I present

to a variety of companies every week. I would never be able to create an entirely new presentation for every conference, and about 80 percent of my content is standardised. As a result, I always personalise the opening. I'll talk about something specifically related to that company so they immediately feel this has been created just for them. I script and learn this opening off by heart because the last thing I want to do is start with a fumble. Occasionally the MC or previous speaker will say something that I want to allude to, in which case I will then mentally script my opening just before I go on stage. This makes it even fresher and more personalised, and the audience knows and appreciates that you're ad-libbing so it doesn't have to be quite as smooth.

While the shocking statement, powerful question and personalised opening are all viable starting options, never start with an introduction or a thank you – this is the quickest way to lose the audience's attention. It's boring and it will make you sound like everyone else. Notice how good newspaper articles start: they get straight to the point.

Of course we may still need introductions. Here's how to get them right.

INTRODUCTIONS

Usually teams introduce themselves before they start, but by the time each person gets to their presentation the buyer is likely to have forgotten who they are. Rather have each person introduced before their section, either by the team leader or the previous presenter.

An introduction is an opportunity to build your value, and getting someone else to do it is preferable for two reasons. It helps avoid the appearance of self-aggrandisement and it offers an opportunity to demonstrate the high regard team members have for one another.

Whether introducing yourself or someone else, avoid the list of boring biographical details. People are less interested in who you are than in what you can do for them, so the best introductions are stories that illustrate your value.

One of the best introductions I've ever received was when the MC didn't mention a single thing about my degrees, accolades or experience; he simply told an anecdote about how I had coached Mode, the startup that went on to win IBM Global Entrepreneur of the Year. He ended by quoting their CEO: 'Justin played an amazing role in making this happen, and we are very excited to attribute a part of our win to the transformation he gave us in our message delivery.' No list of my books or programmes could have better incentivised the audience of entrepreneurs to sit up and listen.

Introductions also give you a standard way to transition from one section to the next.

SIGNPOSTING

A presentation is like a journey. You are the tour guide. You can show me beautiful sites and tell me great stories, but the tour party also needs to be reminded where they are on the tour. We call this signposting.

For instance, let's say your presentation is made up of three key points: passion, partnership and perspective. After your power opening, you could briefly tell us where we're going by mentioning these three points. As you go through the presentation remind us which point you are covering and at the end give us a summary. When I worked as a television producer we had an old saying: 'Tell them what you're going to tell them, then tell them, then tell them what you've told them.' Repetition is the mother of learning. Telling them once will seldom drive home your point sufficiently.

However, you don't always have to fully outline everything up front. For instance, you might say, 'You're about to discover the three Ps to a successful project,' without initially listing all three Ps. This stimulates the audience's curiosity while priming them to look out for those three Ps during the presentation.

CATCHPHRASES

People will remember very little from your presentation. That's human nature. To ensure they remember the most important points, create snappy catchphrases, which are far easier to remember than long, complicated sentences.

Consider, for example, Simon Sinek's famous TED Talk 'How great leaders inspire action', one of the most-viewed in history. Sinek sums up his entire talk in three words: 'Start with why.'[5] More than a phrase, this is a call to action. He repeats it so often that it's almost impossible to forget by the end of it.

Sinek has other memorable sayings that pack a punch. For example, 'People don't buy *what* you do, they buy *why* you do it.' Repeating the word 'buy' and switching 'what' for 'why' uses assonance and alliteration – rhetorical devices that make the phrase catchy.[6] It's not just what we say, it's how we say it. Catchphrases have a musical, rhyming quality that makes them both pleasant to the ear and memorable. Ideally, repeat your central idea as a catchphrase at least three times in your presentation.

Even when you're not using catchphrases, try to keep your sentences short, simple and declarative. The TED Talks provide some of the greatest modern speeches you'll hear, yet the average TED Talk uses language at a 6th-grade level.[7] Follow their example, and convey your message with as little verbiage as possible. Big words, long sentences and jargon don't impress; they confuse listeners and make us sound pompous. As Albert Einstein said, 'You don't really understand something unless you can explain it to your grandmother.'

METAPHOR

A metaphor compares the idea you want to communicate to something more sensory and emotive – or just something better able to communicate your point. When you say that your product is the Rolls-Royce of its category, I immediately know that it's the best available. You're borrowing all the positive attributes of a Rolls-Royce and associating them with your product.

We use metaphors all the time, often without realising it. Do you know what a 'live memory-staging area' is? It's where your emails are

'Metaphors have a way of holding the most truth in the least space.'
– Orson Scott Card

stored. So some bright spark thought to just call it an 'inbox'. How about 'a structured user interaction table'? That's what we call our 'desktop', another metaphor. Translated into old but familiar office features, these complex technological breakthroughs become familiar and accessible. These are metaphors that are so successful they have become neologisms – new words.

Risk Radar is a metaphor for a client of mine's risk assessment tool. Radar detects the variable presence of moving objects. Risk Radar detects the variable presence of risks. What sounds better, Risk Radar or Variable Presence of Risks Detector? The former, not only because it's more succinct and visual, but because it better captures what Risk Radar does.

It's best to choose a metaphor that appeals to your target audience. For instance, if you know they love soccer use a soccer metaphor. But if they are culture-vulture foodies, you're better off finding a comparison from the art or food worlds.

The easiest way to find a metaphor is by asking yourself, 'What is it like?' For example, I offer an anxiety programme that helps to clear the mind of anxious thoughts. What's it like? It's like a 'detox for the brain'. Everyone knows what a physical detox is. By using the term in relation to the mind, it becomes more tangible and desirable.

HUMOUR

There's a running joke on the speaking circuit.

> *Question:* 'Should you put humour in your speech?'
> *Answer:* 'Only if you want to get paid!'

Humour does four important things. First, laughter boosts endorphins, those feel-good brain chemicals. A key to persuasion is liking. The more they like you, the more they want to do business with you. If you're the one who made them laugh, you can be sure they're feeling good about you.

Second, laughter reduces stress hormones like cortisol. A pitch is a high-stress environment. Laughter helps both you and your audience relax.

Third, it keeps people awake. One of the biggest challenges with any presentation is that the audience has to sit still for a long time. Prolonged stillness generally leads to sleep or irritation. Laughter transports fresh flows of oxygen into the brain, enhancing attention.[8]

Finally, when we laugh together we feel united, and the more connected we feel, the more likely we're going to want to do business together.

When it comes to humour, avoid telling a joke that has nothing to do with your content. Rather link humour to enhance, or even make, your point. Google should help if you're struggling to find something appropriate – there are loads of humour sites with funny lines on just about everything. Just be sure to adapt the joke to fit in with your story.

Also avoid risqué humour, especially in our sensitive age. A misfiring joke that offends the wrong person could kill a pitch in an instant. If you're not sure, run it past a few people first.

Humour often uses ridicule, and the safest thing to poke fun at is yourself. In doing so, you have an opportunity to make an important point. For instance, in one pitch I worked on, the leader of the team used this line: 'We could take you through an extensive review of our quality process, but – while we're sure you would find that as riveting as we do – instead we'll just let you know that last year, of the Big Four accounting firms, we were the only one who received "no findings".'

The humour is, of course, in the idea that an extensive review of quality would be riveting to the client when in reality it would bore them to tears. But it also reminds the client they can rest assured that this process, boring to most people, is the team's passion. By making fun of what turns on the audit team, humour avoids what could come across as an arrogant brag – the firm's Number 1 status.

PERSUASIVE LANGUAGE PATTERNS

While stories, slogans, metaphors and humour are all examples of persuasive language, there are specific language patterns that are also important for persuasion.

Some of what I'm about to share may seem counterintuitive. You might wonder how choosing slightly different words can increase buy-in. But when it comes to influence, small things can have big effects. Professor Robert Cialdini, one of the world's leading researchers on influence, explains how we can all be more influential by understanding what ethologists calls **fixed action patterns**.

Cialdini uses the example of the turkey and its natural enemy, the polecat. If a turkey is confronted with even a stuffed polecat, she will peck and claw at it in vicious rage. However, if the stuffed polecat has a recorder inside that makes the same cheep-cheep sound of a baby turkey, she will gather the stuffed polecat underneath her protectively. The cheep-cheep sound is a **trigger feature** – it triggers an automatic mothering response. The trigger feature is often a small part of the total stimulus. When it comes to turkey-mothering, the cheep-cheep sound is more important than anything else.

Human beings also have fixed action patterns. Cialdini cites the work of Harvard social psychologist Ellen Langer. In one study, Langer asked people waiting in a queue for a photocopy machine with the line, 'May I use the machine because I'm in a rush?' Nearly all – 94 percent – of people let her slip ahead. Yet when she simply asked, 'May I use the machine?' without explanation, agreement dropped to 60 percent.

You might think the trigger feature was '... because I'm in a rush'. But Langer showed that this was not the case. In a third scenario she said, 'May I use the machine because I have to make some copies.' Once again nearly all – 93 percent – of people agreed, even though no real new reason or information was provided. The word 'because' triggered what I call an **unconscious compliance response**.

And there is our first lesson in persuasive language patterns: **always provide a reason for action**. Almost any reason is better than no reason.

Language patterns that trigger unconscious compliance responses work precisely because they are unconscious. They are not amenable to the same analysis and scepticism of a logical argument. That's not to say your audience won't analyse the rest of your pitch, but if they find value, these patterns could tip them over the edge. Human beings often find it tough to make decisions. Persuasive language patterns make it easier to make decisions that we are already inclined towards.

Here are six more persuasive language patterns.

'So You Can...'

As we've seen, human beings are motivated by two things: pain and pleasure. We're motivated to reduce pain and increase pleasure. If I am going to adopt your idea or offering, I need to be convinced that it will benefit me by either taking away some pain or providing some pleasure. The key word here is *benefit*. Salespeople often emphasise features of their products when what people are really buying are the benefits.

One way to ensure your language is benefit-oriented is to follow any description of a feature with the words 'so you can...' Don't just tell me the running shoes have an ultra-boost sole with added absorption, tell me that the running shoes have an ultra-boost sole with added absorption *so you can move faster with less chance of injury.*

Likewise, don't just tell your kids to do their homework. Rather say, 'Do your homework *so you can become smarter and then go out to play.*'

Triple Fact

1 You want to get better at pitching.
2 You know this will improve your chance of business success.
3 And you know the best way to get great at pitching is with the Pitch To Win 6-step formula.

The first two statements are almost certainly true – the fact that you're reading this virtually proves them. The third is not as obvious, especially in isolation, but coming after you've agreed to the first two, it carries a lot more credibility. People are more likely to believe something new when it follows from something they already believe. Thus the triple fact is a classic compliance trigger.

You could frame the statements as questions and actually get the audience to say the word 'Yes'. This technique can be even more powerful, but it depends on the nature of the audience. It may work well on junior corporates but a group of high-powered venture capitalists will be less likely to sit there saying 'yes' in unison.

'If You're Someone...'

People feel compelled to believe and act in line with their identity. Here you link what you want them to believe to their self-image.

Which of these two statements is more convincing?

1 You need this programme to help you make more sales.

2 If you're someone who can really help people and deliver real value, you're going to want this programme to help you make more sales.

The key words in the second statement are 'If you're someone...' If you follow with a description that fits their self-image – most people see themselves as helpful – they are more likely to believe the linked statement.

'You...'

The brain will almost only ever follow through on a decision if it can visualise a positive outcome. By using language that enables the prospect to see themselves using your offering, you increase the chances of them buying. The key word here is 'you'. Note the link to second-person storytelling discussed earlier.

Compare the following:

1 The Super Suck Vacuum Cleaner sucks up twice as much dirt.

2 When *you* clean your house with the Super Suck Vacuum Cleaner *you* will suck up twice as much dirt.

With the second statement the potential buyers can see themselves using your product.

This One or That One

Remember the reactance effect? It's our aversion to overt persuasion. When we're feeling pushed to do something, our instinctive response is often to refuse. No-one likes feeling like they don't have a choice. Related to this, we also don't like having just one choice. There is even a term for this: **single-option aversion**.

When consumers could choose between two brands of DVD player rather than one, sales increased by 34 percent.[9] However it can also be frustrating to have to choose between two equally attractive options, which is why it's better to make one more attractive than the other. What you don't want is too many options. That confuses the brain and it becomes easier not to buy.

Clearly / Obviously / Everybody

Words like *clearly*, *obviously* or *everybody* trigger compliance by removing doubt. When you tell me that something is 'obvious' or 'everyone knows', I am likely to assume there is no reason to question it. Of course, there is a limit to this. If I tell you that you should '*obviously* sign over your life savings to me' or '*everybody* believes my product is the best', you're unlikely to fall for it. You only use this compliance trigger to add persuasive power to something that others would probably agree with.

These techniques can seem manipulative, but we're not turkeys and polecats. Rather than *fixed action patterns*, it may be better to say that human beings have **default action patterns**. In the absence of compelling alternative options, we will tend to comply with these triggers.

But remember: humans almost always have alternative options. If you aren't offering genuine value, none of this is likely to work – and if it does, they'll soon leave when they discover the truth.

VISUAL AIDS

The nerves dedicated to auditory processing take up just 3 percent of our brain's cortex. Nerves dedicated to visual processing take up 30 percent.[10] That tells you just how important visuals can be. But always remember: the most important visual in the room is not the PowerPoint slides; it's you!

Have you noticed that when you read or hear a good story your mind creates a rich visual world to match? You vividly see the places, people and objects that are described. This can be even more powerful than watching a movie because these self-generated images are deeply personal; they connect to your own history and experience.

Sometimes when I arrive for a keynote presentation without a laptop and my client asks me for my PowerPoint presentation I tell them, 'I'm the power point.' I'm confident

'PowerPoint is for people with no power and no point.'
– Anonymous

that my non-verbal communication – my body language; much of what we've been discussing here – will provide the visual power I need. Having said that, I do occasionally use external visuals, and I recommend their judicious use to inexperienced presenters in particular. When visuals truly support your message, retention of your message three days later can, according to one study, be increased by more than 50 percent.[11] This is because the brain thinks largely in pictures.

The use of slides does, however, come with potential pitfalls. The biggest mistake I see people make is putting their speech notes on the projector. Slide after slide of extensive bullet points are usually there to remind the presenter of what they need to say. Avoid this. If you need to be reminded, hold those notes in front of you. Shoving them in front of the audience will do three things: bore them with the extensive lecture they think they're about to get, overwhelm them with too much information and, worst of all, pull attention away from you, the speaker. I can't look at you *and* reams of text. And when I don't look at you our rapport is broken. Remember, eye contact is one of the keys to building trust and liking with your audience. While I'm looking at the screen, I'm certainly not looking in your eyes.

When I do use visuals, I try to include on each slide no more than an image along with a word or phrase that summarises that particular part of the presentation. The word or phrase serves as a reminder to the audience of the main point. The image brings it to life. Finally, I may put up a summary slide of the three to five main points of the entire presentation.

Bear in mind that digital slides are not the only way to go. With smaller, boardroom-style audiences you could also use placemats, easels with printed paper that you write on or flip over, or even physical objects like puzzles. Physical objects add a tactile dimension, making you and your message more memorable. But these can't just be used for surprise value; they need to add to your message.

CLOSING

After your opening, your closing is more important than anything else.

> 'All's well that ends well.'
> – William Shakespeare

In clinical studies it's been shown that if a colonoscopy ends painfully, the entire procedure will be remembered as painful and unpleasant. However, once it is over, if the doctor pretends it's still continuing for a few minutes, without pain, the patient will remember the entire procedure as far less painful and more bearable. Yet the same amount of pain was delivered; it was just the ending that differed.

The end characterises the whole. Just think of a gripping thriller with a lame ending; you're likely to remember the whole film as a dud.

You could end with a short, final story that encapsulates your key idea, or a brief summary of your key points. But in most pitches you will end with a call to action.

The Call To Action

Whether it's five minutes or an hour, by the end of your pitch, you've hopefully got your audience primed to feel excited about all the value you can bring them. Feelings are not stable. They are fleeting. You want to leverage that feeling right there and then by getting them to commit to action.

Usually people don't give a call to action for two reasons. First, because they're scared of being rejected. But a refusal to act should not be considered a rejection, it's just an objection. If your prospects resist taking action, ask them what their objection is and tell them how you can overcome it. Far worse if you think it went well, they don't buy, and you never find out what was holding them back.

The second reason we usually don't give a call to action is the belief that if our prospective clients like what they've heard they'll buy without us asking them to. This is sometimes true, but research shows that people are more likely to buy when they're explicitly told what to do.

We're all inundated with information and easily distracted. No matter how compelling your proposition, when your audience leave the room they're probably going to stop thinking about you and start thinking about their next obligation. From there, the memory of you and your offering only dims. If they've made a commitment, however small, whether signing a form or just setting up another meeting, they can't forget you.

Ideally the call to action should:

1 Be something they can do right now.
2 Be easy to do.
3 Feel like a natural next step.

The only time this might not be appropriate is if you're pitching alongside other candidates. Telling them to sign up now may come across as pushy or arrogant. In that case, make sure that your final sentences are a passionate reminder of all the value they will get by choosing you.

THE Q&A

Do you think you're more likely to be persuaded by listening to someone give a speech or by having a conversation with them? The speech may impress you but it takes the conversation to convince you. A Q&A achieves this in three ways.

First, it shows that you're agile. You're not just an automaton who's learnt a speech; you have intimate knowledge of your topic and you're able to think on your feet. Second, it enables you to address the most critical concerns of the audience that you may not have covered. Finally, by engaging in a conversation, you can build a deeper rapport.

Instead of seeing them as a test, **see questions as an opportunity to sell or resell the benefits of what you're offering**. If there is anything bothering your potential clients, you want to know about it now so that you can address it.

Q&A 10-POINT GUIDELINE

1. Create a list of likely, less likely and challenging questions. Specifically consider questions you would *not* want to be asked.
2. Debate the answers with your team.
3. Decide who will answer what question.
4. Rehearse your answers but don't learn them off by heart. This section needs to be conversational. Have faith in your knowledge and experience.
5. If you're not sure you've understood the question, ask for clarification.
6. If you're asked a question with an answer that has been rehearsed by another team member, refer it to that person.
7. Reframe negative questions into positive responses. As in the example on p31, if you're questioned about a lack of experience, don't be defensive and deny the charge; rather acknowledge their

legitimate concern and then talk about the experience you do have.

8 Keep your answers simple and concise. Don't waffle in the hope that you'll cover what they want to know. Make a clear point, and if you're unsure if you've adequately answered their question, ask, 'Does that answer your question?'

9 If you don't know the answer to a question, you can look to one of your colleagues, but if no-one knows the answer don't pretend you do. Acknowledge the value of the question and promise to return after the pitch with the answer.

10 Never end the presentation with a Q&A. If you get a negative or bland question this will be the last thing your audience remembers. Rather repeat your closing remarks or provide a new closing. This could also be the time to bring in your call to action.

WRITTEN vs. ORAL PRESENTATIONS

Too often the written and oral presentations are created separately, even by different sets of people. The one should be a direct reflection of the other.

Once the pitch team have created their oral

presentation, this should be used as a basis for the written proposal. That way there is a consistent message. And there is nothing wrong with repeating key points and stories from the oral proposal in the written version. Repetition is one of the keys to persuasion: the more we are exposed to a message, the more it has the ring of truth.

The written proposal will provide more information, some of it mandatory and standardised, such as general processes and procedures. This is important, but note that a survey of 70 top European companies on the reasons for choosing a winning pitch placed the written proposal as the tenth and last reason. The written proposal is, therefore, more of a potential banana peel than anything else: while it probably won't win you the bid, if it's sloppy, incomplete or contains errors, it could lose it.

REHEARSAL

Once you have a presentation, do you learn it off by heart? As a conference speaker I can tell you there are no rules on this. Some of my successful colleagues learn key points and improvise around them. Others write a script and learn it off by heart. They are still able to veer off script if they need to, but they learn it almost like an actor learns their lines. I prefer the latter for two reasons.

First, if you don't learn it off by heart, you may waffle or simply not say it as well on show day. Second, you're likely to be more nervous if you're not entirely sure what's coming out of your mouth.

The two potential disadvantages of learning it off by heart are: it can sound fake or over-rehearsed if it gets too slick; and if you forget your words or get interrupted with a question, you may find yourself stumbling into an awkward silence. Both of those disadvantages can, however, be prevented in the way that you learn your script.

REHEARSAL 10-POINT GUIDELINE

1 Write your script in colloquial language. Avoid formal, literary turns of phrase. As you write it, speak it out to hear if it sounds natural to the ear.

2 Be clear about the key points, so that if you're interrupted or forget your words you're still able to talk about them.

3 Memorise your speech out loud. If you do it in your head your brain will remember it as an internal process rather than an external speech.

4 Memorise each paragraph at a time. Don't move on to the next paragraph until you've memorised the previous one.

5 To remember how to link from one paragraph to the next, create an association in your mind that links the last idea of the previous paragraph to the first idea of the next. For example, if the first paragraph ends with the name of their company and the next paragraph starts with yours, in your mind link their company to yours.

6 Practise vocalising your speech with all the body language and vocal expression and projection you will use on show day. Your brain will now associate what you say with how you say it. Also, by moving while you memorise your script, you oxygenate your brain, facilitating learning.

7 If you're not going to memorise the whole script, at least memorise the beginning and the end so that you start and finish flawlessly, on a punch.

8 There is nothing wrong with having a small piece of paper that fits into the palm of your hand with the key point of each paragraph as reminders. Avoid taking the whole speech with you: you will be tempted to simply read it.

9 Rehearse a few times in front of a mirror or, better yet, film yourself. You will often pick up things that need to change when you can see yourself in action.

10 Rehearse in front of an audience so you can take feedback from your colleagues.

IN CONCLUSION

That concludes the TTOPPS formula: your six keys to a winning pitch:

T	Tune in
T	Team
O	Optimism
P	Presence
P	Purpose
S	Story

In your next pitch may you create a powerful **team**, brimming with **optimism**, vibrating with **presence** and driven by **purpose**, to deliver a riveting **story**!

Time for my own call to action: let's stay in touch! Sign up for my blog at **www.justinpresents.com**. Even better, join me for a Pitch To Win Master Class by going to **www.pitchtowin.live**. And if you're looking for training, coaching or a Pitch To Win presentation for your organisation, send an email to **info@ justinpresents.com**. Finally, if you have a Pitch To Win success story, we'd love to hear about it.

Now, get out there and pitch to win!

REFERENCES

Introduction

1 'Teaching Sales' by Suzanne Fogel, David Hoffmeister, Richard Rocco and Daniel P Struck, *Harvard Business Review* (July-August, 2012)

2 *Mindset: The new psychology of success* by C Dweck (Ballantine, 2007)

3 *Peak* by A Ericsson and R Pool (Eamon Dolan/Mariner Books, 2016)

Chapter 1

1 *Influence* by R Cialdini (Harper Business, 2006)

2 *Give And Take* by A Grant (Penguin, 2014)

3 *To Sell Is Human* by P Daniel (Riverhead Books, 2013)

4 'Personality And Performance At The Beginning Of The New Millennium: What do we know and where do we go next?' By Murray R Barrick, Michael K Mount and Timothy A Judge, *International Journal Of Selection And Assessment*, 9 (March-June, 2001)

Chapter 2

1 *The Happiness Advantage* by S Achor (Crown Business, 2010)

2 'Positive Affect Facilitates Integration Of Information And Decreases Anchoring In Reasoning Among Physicians' by CA Estrada, AM Isen and MJ Young, *Organizational Behavior And Human Decision Processes* (1997)

3 *On Becoming A Person* by C Rogers (Robinson, 2004)

Chapter 3

1 *Learned Optimism* by M Selgman (Vintage Books, 2006)

2 'What Is Fatigue?' by Alex Hutchinson, www.newyorker.com/tech/elements/what-is-fatigue (December, 2014)

3 'What Breaking The 4-Minute Mile Taught Us About The Limits Of Conventional Thinking' by Bill Taylor, *Harvard Business Review* (9 March 2018)

4   *Give And Take* by A Grant (Penguin, 2014)

5   'Why We Win And Why We Lose', EY Study (2016)

Chapter 4

1   *Nonverbal Communication* by A Mehrabian (Aldine-Atherton, 1972)

2   'The Communication Of Friendly And Hostile Attitudes By Verbal And Non-verbal Signals' by M Argyle, F Alkema and R Gilmour, *European Journal of Social Psychology* (July 1971)

3   www.fau.edu/newsdesk/articles/Voice%20Pitch-Study.php

4   'Nonverbal Behavior And The Theory Of Emotion: The facial feedback hypothesis' by R Buck, *Journal Of Personality And Social Psychology*, 38 (5): 813 (1980)

5   'Looking And Loving: The effect of mutual gaze on feelings of romantic love' by J Kellerman, J Lewis and JD Laird, *Journal Of Research In Personality*, 23 (1989)

6   'Direct Look Versus Evasive Glance And Compliance With A Request' by N Guegen and C Jacob, *The Journal Of Social Psychology* (July 2000)

7   'Your Body Language Shapes Who You Are' by A Cuddy (TED Talk, June 2012)

8   'Hand, Mouth And Brain' by Jana M Iverson and Esther Thelen, *Journal of Consciousness Studies* (2005)

9   *To Sell Is Human* by P Daniel (Riverhead Books, 2013)

10   *Give And Take* by A Grant (Penguin, 2014)

11   *To Sell Is Human* by P Daniel (Riverhead Books, 2013)

12   'The Thing We Fear More Than Death' by G Croston, *Psychology Today* (November 2012)

13   *The Relaxation Response* by H Benson (Harper Torch, 2000)

14   'How To Make Stress Your Friend' by Kelly McGonigal (TED Talk, June 2013)

15   *The Power Of Habit* by Charles Duhigg (Corner Stone Digital, 2012)

Chapter 5

1   *To Sell Is Human* by P Daniel (Riverhead Books, 2013)
2   *Give And Take* by A Grant (Penguin, 2014)

Chapter 6

1   http://www.fmcg.ie/product-sampling-on-the-increase/
2   *The Astonishing Power Of Story* by Justin Cohen (Wordout Publishing, 2009)
3   *Made To Stick* by Chip Heath and Dan Heath (Random House, 2008)
4   *The Fourth Industrial Revolution* by K Schwab (World Economic Forum, 2016)
5   'How Great Leaders Inspire Action' by Simon Sinek (TED Talk, September 2009)
6   'How Great Leaders Inspire Action' by Simon Sinek (TED Talk, September 2009)
7   *How To Deliver A TED Talk* by J Donovan (McGraw-Hill Education, 2013)
8   *Laughter, The Best Medicine* by R Holden (Thorsons, 1993)
9   'Single-option Aversion' by Daniel Mochon, *Journal of Consumer Research*, 40 (October 2013); 'Research Watch', *Harvard Business Review* (October 2013)
10 *Metaphorically Selling* by A Miller (Chiron Associates, 2004)
11 Medina, *Brain Rules*, 234

ACKNOWLEDGEMENTS

Thank you to John Sanei for showing me what a business book should look like, and then introducing me to Tim Richman and his team at Burnet Media to execute it. Tim, your attention to detail and your uncomplaining acceptance of my last-minute revisions makes you, to me at least, the patron saint of publishing. Finally, Noa De Bruyn, thank you for believing in Pitch To Win from the beginning, and reminding me that there is no reason to play small.

 JustinPresents
f @JustinPresents
 @JustinPresents
 www.justinpresents.com
